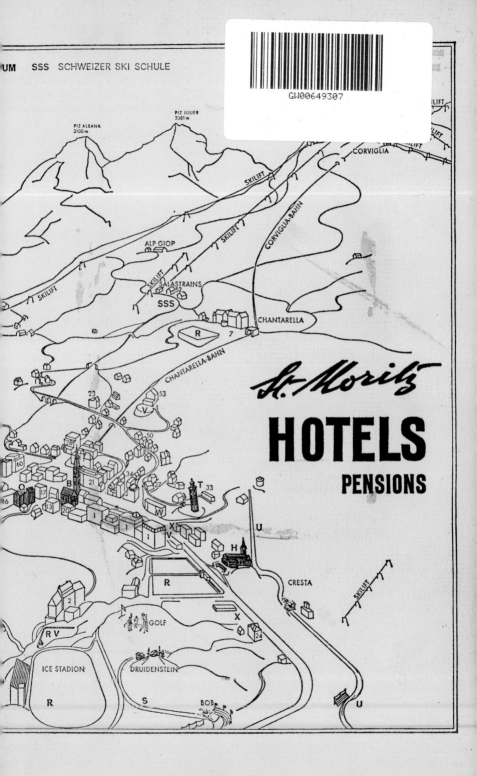

St. Moritz

HOTELS
PENSIONS

St Moritz

An Alpine Capriccio

By the same author

The Winning Counter : Hugh Fraser and Harrods
Muirfield and the Honourable Company

George Pottinger

St Moritz
An Alpine Caprice

 Jarrolds, London

JARROLDS PUBLISHERS (LONDON) LTD
3 Fitzroy Square, London W1

AN IMPRINT OF THE HUTCHINSON GROUP

London Melbourne Sydney Auckland
Wellington Johannesburg Cape Town
and agencies throughout the world

First published 1972

*This book has been designed and produced by Hutchinson Benham Ltd,
set in Imprint type, printed in Great Britain on antique wove paper
by Anchor Press, and bound by Wm. Brendon, both of Tiptree, Essex*

ISBN 0 09 111330 X

CONTENTS

For Meg and Piers

ILLUSTRATIONS

From Muottas Muragl to the Roseg Valley and Piz Palu

Acknowledgements

The illustrations listed above are all from the collection in the
St Moritz Kurverein Library. Some are of unknown origin but
acknowledgements are due to:

A. Pedrett, St Moritz; Foto Max, St Moritz; Foto Plattner, St
Moritz; L. Hauri, St Moritz; Rutz, St Moritz; Lamberto Londi,
Milan; Keystone, Zürich; Dr. Rudolf H. Schloss, Zürich; Desmond
O'Neill, England; Swiss National Tourist Office, Zürich.

FOREWORD BY
SIR HUGH FRASER, Bart.

I am glad to have the opportunity of providing a foreword to *St Moritz*. Bearing in mind the favoured place which St Moritz has long held in our affections and our known addiction to travel literature and the accounts of early voyagers, it is surprising that, so far as is known, no comprehensive account of St Moritz and its own mystique has yet appeared in English. George Pottinger's book remedies this deficiency.

All the elements which go to make up the St Moritz legend are clearly delineated. There were the first visitors who came to take the cure at the mineral springs. Then came Johannes Badrutt's famous bet last century when the far-seeing hotelier overcame the disbelief of a party of English visitors and proved that St Moritz had an even more pleasant climate in the winter than in the summer. This led in turn to successive waves of tourists, with the English usually in the majority. The formation of St Moritz's own specialties, the Cresta and bob runs, and—surprisingly, very much later—the rise of ski-ing as much the most popular pastime, followed. More recently other forms of tourist development, sometimes a daunting phrase, have been carried out with taste and distinction.

This by itself makes a good story, and the impact of the English on the orderly growth from an Alpine village to one of the most *recherché* of European resorts is always of interest. For the first time, too, the history of St Moritz in all its aspects is set in the general Swiss context with a great deal of information which is not generally available in English. But it is in his exposition of what he terms 'the high life proper' that the author's real originality lies. The book describes the different classes of society and the personalities who have contributed to the various seasons at St Moritz. And the conclusion that the high life is both a hoax and a reality which can be enjoyed by everyone who goes there is an engrossing one. Future sociologists may find this an unexpected starting point.

My own interest in the village is of long standing and dates from the time some years ago when my father took his family there on the first of many holidays. He always maintained that nowhere else could he find such relaxation and exhilaration. After his first visit he returned almost annually during January and February and he found St Moritz's charm so magnetic that he frequently made his way there for a few days in the summer as well. The sharp, clear air of the Engadine Valley, the sense of sitting perched on the cross-roads of Europe, the agreeable company of others clearly enjoying themselves, all these he said were better at St Moritz than elsewhere. And in this, as in many other matters, I have never doubted his wisdom.

There is a further theme in this book which I find of peculiar interest. This is that at St Moritz the near prospect of high moun-tains induces more thoughtfulness and more engaging reveries than might be expected on what is basically an extrovert holiday. Of course, a stay there is escapist; but is a few weeks' break from the daily routine any the worse for that? It adds to both the relaxation and the exhilaration.

My father found much at St Moritz that could be identified and relived in the Scottish Highlands when he planned his pleasant place of festivity at Aviemore. The author is well aware of this and his account is both amusing and authoritative. Nothing else would have done for the spirit of St Moritz.

Dineiddwg,
1972

AUTHOR'S PREFACE

Who would not rejoice at the chance to write about something he really enjoys? I enjoy St Moritz and in this book I have tried to capture what, for me, are its main attractions and what makes it so memorably different from other places. If the result has not turned out to be an orthodox history or travel guide but has emerged as something much more eclectic, this simply exemplifies the village's ubiquitous charm.

Anyone who writes about the Swiss mountains must begin by paying tribute to the work of the three great British Alpinists Sir Leslie Stephen, Sir Gavin de Beer and, above all, Sir Arnold Lunn who has assured himself immortality by his contribution to British ski-ing. I do so willingly.

I have been greatly fortified by the assistance readily given to me by a number of fellow enthusiasts. First, Herr Peter Kasper and his staff at the St Moritz Kurverein have gone out of their way to elicit all the information I wanted. Without their help this book would not have been possible. When it was necessary they prised details from the St Moritz hoteliers and they have also provided the inspired collection of photographs from their own library. Others who have been particularly helpful include Mr W. D. Cormack; Mr Robin Welsh, the Secretary of the Royal Caledonian Curling Club; Sir James Corry, the President, and Mrs Max Jaffa, the Honorary Secretary, of the St Moritz Curling Club; Mr Kenneth Dilnott Cooper, the senior statesman of ski racing; and two well-known Scottish bobbers, Mr Frank Usher and Mr Tony Fyldes. Mr Edward Kemp, Curator at the Royal Botanic Garden, Edinburgh; Miss C. L. Dickson of the Edinburgh Central Library; and the staff of the Scottish National Library: all were unremitting in providing assistance.

I am happy to acknowledge Mr Sandy Wilson's kindness in allowing me to reproduce the song from *Valmouth*. I hope that those who read this book will agree that at St Moritz, at any rate, all that silk and satin gear are still needed and these dancing days are not yet gone.

Gullane,
1972

I

Of the Swiss

St Moritz has long been cherished by the English as one of their favourite places, but they have not written much about it. Earlier Alpine writers—starting in the eighteenth century with Joseph Addison, who declared that the mountains 'fill the mind with an agreeable kind of horror', down to John Ruskin with his Gothic theories and, more recently, Sir Arnold Lunn—have all been more concerned with the really majestic peaks and with the unmistakable drama of high places than with the urbane and graceful happenings in the Upper Engadine. As a result, St Moritz qualifies for only an incidental mention, as a kind of staging post, in most Alpine literature.

My affection for St Moritz dates from long before my first visit. In the hot, dry summer of 1945, stationed in Italy on the shores of the Adriatic like most of the remnants of the Eighth Army, we lay languidly on the beaches guarding prisoners of war and waiting for repatriation. The general malaise and anti-climax were diversified by an ingenuous staff officer at H.Q. Eighth Army who ordained that in preparation for their return to civilian life soldiers were to be given training in self-reliance. For this pompous purpose they should go on short journeys, lasting for several days, without supervision. We gladly interpreted his decree as authorising the despatch of 15 cwt trucks containing parties of six gunners with all the pay they could draw, a week's rations, and a copy of the historic Eighth Army letter to prove they were not deserters. They could have a

15

week's holiday anywhere they liked, and the only requirement was to bring the trucks back undamaged.

The first party went straight over the Alps by a route that might have made even Hannibal incredulous. They drove a clumsy, war-weary vehicle; they writhed over gorges; they did everything except blow up rocks with vinegar like the hero of Carthage. They came back after a week in Switzerland. 'You're right, sir. The war is over.' They had come to rest in the Engadine Valley and after three days in an hotel at St Moritz had fearfully asked for the bill, wondering whether a quick getaway might be needed. The hotelier brought them a formidable-looking account, lengthy and Germanic in appearance, and an extra glass of kirsch. (After living too long on the sickly Italian liqueurs of Strega and Fiore delle Alpi they soon found the sharper taste of the Swiss elixir acceptable.) When they had examined the details the landlord took back the bill and tore it up. 'This is what you might pay when you come back. But I would accept no payment from soldiers who have fought for Europe.' They were not the first veterans to rejoice in the goodwill of the Swiss.

It is sometimes the practice to refer reverently to Portugal as our oldest ally, but only Sir Arnold Lunn has remarked that Switzerland is both our oldest non-ally and our oldest non-enemy. We have never fought alongside or against Switzerland, but her neutrality, and in our case it has always been benevolent neutrality, has always been to Europe's advantage. Two world wars have given this added point. In the first, prisoners who were wounded or gravely ill were interned in Switzerland and the Swiss were never backward in sharing their hardships. In the second war the chief belligerent in the Allied cause endorsed this view. In a minute to the Foreign Secretary on 3rd December 1944 Winston Churchill wrote:

> I put this down for the record. Of all neutrals Switzerland has the greatest right to distinction. She has been the sole international force linking the hideously sundered nations

and ourselves. . . . She has been a democratic State, standing for freedom in self-defence among her mountains, and in thought, in spite of race, largely on our side.

So this is inevitably a book not only about St Moritz but about Switzerland also, or at least those aspects of the country which are essential to a full enjoyment and understanding of the fundamental and pervasive attraction of the Upper Engadine. Those who arrive in the Happy Valley nowadays, whether majestically by private jet, efficiently by chartered aircraft, or in a more mundane way by train from Zürich, cannot really look at St Moritz *in vacuo*.

There are many aspects of Switzerland which are frequently admired. It is not only, as Sir Leslie Stephen called it, the playground of Europe: it has many other virtues. The first revolt against the rule of feudal lords and the setting up of a rudimentary democracy—early and in European terms a pioneer—followed the defeat of the Habsburgs in a small Swiss mountain pass. They share their property individually in a manner more tolerant and civilised than anything the most radical planners have attempted elsewhere. They keep an admirable balance of power between legitimate local demands in the cantons and the more tight-lipped Federal Government, a balance greatly coveted by nationalist parties elsewhere in Europe and particularly in Great Britain; and their banking and monetary system is said to be so powerful that governments tremble at the first whimper from the Gnomes of Zürich. None of these is our primary concern.

But we are concerned with the impact which Switzerland has made on men's minds. The first thing that has struck visitors, whether or not affected by any fashionable aesthetic movement, has always been the unrelieved grandeur of the high mountains. This has had an effect which supersedes normal reaction. (It would, on the whole, be necessary to go to the Himalayas, or South America, to find any other ranges which would so stun the intellect by their sheer physical attraction.) The very

B

immensity of the Alps was the quality which struck the best-known Alpinists in English literature: Dorothy Wordsworth, perhaps the most perceptive of all; her brother William; Byron, who saw the Alps through the same distorting perspective as he saw most natural objects; Shelley, who was not really involved; and Ruskin, the great Alpine author who found in the high hills the justification for many of his most advanced theories.

Other writers have been struck by different aspects. The Countess Blessington noted with keen interest the rosy colour which the Alps assume in the evenings. This refined quality of light seems peculiar to the High Alps. In the same way a strange atmospheric condition sometimes occurs in Athens when the very air seems violet coloured, to the wonder of those who are lucky enough to see it from the heights of the Acropolis. It is easy to select examples where writers have symbolised their own aspirations, political, social or romantic, in particular heights. But although the glories of the Alps are frequently evoked in prose and verse, they have seldom been brought within the artist's frame. It is not difficult to see why. Although mountains feature prominently in many of the paintings inspired by the Romantic Revival, the Alps are too big to be brought with credibility within the scope of a normal landscape painting. There are other problems, too. There is the evanescent effect of changing light on the Alpine peaks which poses an almost insoluble problem for the artist; and snow, which most people associate with the Alps, does not lend itself easily to treatment in oils. There are admittedly honourable exceptions, perhaps less known than they ought to be. There is a small esoteric school known as the Swiss Kleinmeisters whose prints (about the end of the eighteenth century) succeed in a totally unspoiled way in catching the essence of the Swiss landscape. They have some English counterparts in the small school of water-colourists of roughly the same period, whose main figures were William Pars, John Robert Cozens and Francis Towne. And, lastly, there is the great Italian painter of the nineteenth century, Segantini, whose heroic attempts to capture space can be seen in the gallery of the St Moritz Museum that bears his name.

It is, however, easier to build or depict a man-made pinnacle —like the Campanile which stretches out from the earth in the Piazza il Campo at Siena—than to capture the grandeur of mountain peaks reaching to the clouds.

For all those who go to Switzerland some appreciation of Swiss history adds to their enjoyment. This is particularly so for the English, since there are many aspects which have provoked their own reaction in England or have themselves influenced contemporary English thought. Switzerland offers an unspoiled, but not a virgin, landscape and the visitor knows that wherever he goes in Switzerland he is in the heart of Europe, European civilisation and European history. He knows that the Alpine passes have been trodden by generals and emperors—Hannibal, Caesar and Napoleon; and that Popes and pilgrims, too, have traversed its territory. An informed appreciation of some of the main events of the past enables him to identify himself more closely with the landscape and with those who have been there before him.

Thomas Cook came comparatively late on the Swiss scene, and even later to St Moritz. His brother acted as Cook's courier at Basle, but this was as far as the firm's organisation had penetrated by the 1870s. His version of the origin of the friendly Swiss is more naïve than his normal utterances. *Cook's Tourist Handbook for 1879* records that:

> Not in the pages of the historian, but beneath the surface of her lakes, are found the earliest records of human existence in the country now called Switzerland. As we shall have occasion to show hereafter, the earliest inhabitants seem to have been a mysterious race, who dwelt in houses reared on piles above the waters of the lakes, and who used stone where we should now use metal.

So mystical an approach is doubtfully necessary, and it is

easier to concentrate on some of the main features which concern the Anglo-Saxons.

The first crucial event in domestic Swiss history was the formation of the Swiss Confederation in 1291 when three of the four Forest Cantons concluded a perpetual League. Not long after, the Confederation took on the full might of the Habsburgs —whose rule had been tolerated because it was imposed fairly lightly and, even more important, from a distance—and won an astounding victory in the narrow defile at Morgarten in 1315. This, the first successful challenge to feudal autocracy, was reinforced by further victories at Sempach (1380) and Nafels (1388). There followed a succession of battles against Charles the Bold of Burgundy at Grandson (1476), Morat in the same year, and Nancy. From then on it was fair to regard Switzerland as the first democratic State in Europe: a democracy based for the most part on rural peasantry which, in a surprisingly disciplined way, was prepared to bear arms and maintain its own militia.

The new democratic concept made a further advance before the end of the century when in 1498 the Grisons became allied with the seven Eastern Cantons of the Confederation and defeated in 1499 the Emperor Maximilian at the historic battle of Calven Gorge. The Emperor failed in his invasion of the Engadine because the Rhaetians burned Zuoz, Samaden, Pontresina and St Moritz (the first mention of the village in modern European history) rather than let the territory fall into his possession. The Emperor made peace at Basle a year later and effectively conceded that from then on Switzerland was no longer part of his empire.

The part which Switzerland played in inspiring the Reformation, and in preserving its principles, and the massive personal contribution of Calvin and Zwingli, belong to ecclesiastical history and have been too often rehearsed to need further exposition here. The same is true of Jean Jacques Rousseau, who has claims to the direct ancestry of the French Revolution.

Archdeacon Coxe, in his famous four journeys through

Switzerland in the decade from 1776 to 1786, found that the Swiss Confederation, by now thirteen cantons, and the various allied independent States, such as the Grisons, had now almost reached the same stage of democratic freedom, but that their problems in administration remained local, for each had their own currency and customs laws, and they all bore arms in their own interest. The time had almost arrived for a further step towards unification. Before this, however, the French revolutionary armies invaded Switzerland in the classic manner, as self-styled liberators, and occupied Berne in 1798. The French proceeded to impose the 'Helvetic' constitution based on a rigid concentration of power in the centre, and utterly foreign to the grass-roots type of constitution which had emerged in the cantons. Switzerland was not to regain its independence until after the defeat of Napoleon in 1812, and Stratford Canning, the newly appointed English ambassador, arrived in Zürich in 1814, much to the satisfaction of the Swiss.

There were two other events which involved England in Swiss history. In 1847 civil war broke out between the Federal Government and the 'Sonderbund', a league of Catholic cantons. Unlike other European countries, England, on Palmerston's advice, made it clear that she would not interfere, and left the Federal Government to prevail. The last occasion when the English were directly involved in Swiss affairs was in 1857 when she supported Switzerland at the conference to settle the Neuchâtel question—a complicated succession dispute which would require a volume in itself to unravel.

It is the English whom we have mentioned so far, although Great Britain was the country involved in these diplomatic exchanges, for it is the English who have always been most affected by Switzerland. Not that the Scots regard themselves as cut off from Switzerland: curling, as we will see, was a native sport in Scotland long before it reached the Engadine; and the Scots, too, are a mountain race. Neither country would have enjoyed the characteristic spleen of Shelley's friend, Thomas Jefferson Hogg, who sneered that:

Switzerland is the Scotland of Europe; a land that supplies servants—a land to be boasted of by its inhabitants, and quitted. The Swiss, like the Scotch, are all of good families, and of old families; I should like much to see a person from either nation of a bad family.

Condescending from the heights of the general Swiss conspectus to the canton where St Moritz lies, the Grisons, or Graubunden, is the farthest east of the Swiss cantons and dates from 1803 when it joined the Swiss Federation. The term 'Grisons' has been interpreted as coming from the word for 'grey', referring to the homespun cloth worn by the local inhabitants, and with some connection with the historic League formed in 1399 called the Oberbund, or Grey League: but the philology is suspect. It seems more likely that the derivation is not from 'grey', but from 'graven', or 'counts', referring to the nobles who formed the League. It is a particularly hilly canton with many glaciers. The chief sources of the Rhine, and source streams which eventually reach the Italian rivers Po and Adige, also come from the Grisons. It contains some of the highest valleys in Central Europe and, in Juf (6998 ft.), the highest village in the Alps which is permanently inhabited. It is not all bleak, however, and below Chur, the capital of the canton, one of the best Swiss wines is produced; and there are chestnuts and mineral springs. In the lower valleys, too, there are pastures of the kind normally associated with Swiss cantonal life.

Throughout the canton the inhabitants are likely to speak Romansch, a language which is singularly confusing for those who are not born with it. Romansch survives in the Grisons, in the Dolomites of the Southern Tyrol and in the Italian province of Udine. There are two variants: Rhaeto-Romansch, which is found principally in the valley of the Rhine and its tributaries; and Ladin, which is much spoken in the Engadine. Romansch speakers proudly claim that their language is not merely a mixture of Italian and German but one in its own right. In the

Grisons, Romansch has for long been a legally admitted language of the canton and, since a memorable plebiscite in 1938, it has been recognised as the fourth national language of Switzerland. Originally Romansch was very much an oral language and the first flowering of its literature dates from the sixteenth century. The first complete Romansch Bible, published at Chur in 1718, was, improbably, dedicated to George II (then Prince of Wales) who graciously recognised the honour which had been conferred on him by a gift of fifty guineas. The word 'Rhaeto', applied to Romansch, comes from the old Roman province of Rhaetia, of which the Grisons was part. Rhaetia suffered like other former Roman domains under the Ostrogoths and the Franks, but after the time of Charlemagne was ruled by the Bishops of Chur. By the twelfth century the Chur bishops had developed a growing appetitite for temporal power and allied themselves to the Habsburgs. Resentment at the increasing power of the bishops led to the creation of another Swiss alliance—the League of God's House, or the Gotteshausbund—which was to survive in one form or another until 1801, when the Grisons was compelled to join the Helvetic Republic. Soon afterwards the canton of Grisons became part of the Swiss Confederation and has so remained.

Within the Grisons, the Engadine Valley extends for sixty miles from Martinsbruck in the north-east to the Maloja plateau in the south-west and includes the Sils, Silvaplana and St Moritz lakes. Engadine comes from the Romansch 'Engiadina', which means 'at the head of the Inn', or, in the original, *'En cha d'En in capeti Oeni'*. Bounded by steep mountain passes on all sides, the valley is still surprisingly wide and open (sometimes up to eight miles across), which gives many more hours of sunshine in winter than would normally be expected at this altitude. The impression of a mountain fastness, peculiar to the Upper Engadine, is reinforced by the nature of the approach routes. The summits of the main passes are all so high that a considerable amount of activity is required to keep them open all winter. Especially on a first visit there is a sense of excitement in surmounting one of the passes before descending to the valley. Taken in order, the routes are, first, over the Maloja (5961 ft.) from Lake Como to Chiavenna through the beautiful Val Bregaglia, with a great clutch of hairpin bends before the summit is reached. Next there is the impressive Julier from Tiefencastel to the Engadine, perhaps the most historic of all the approach routes and one that features prominently in our story. Then there is the Albula (7595 ft.) as an alternative from Chur; and, lastly, the Bernina (7645 ft.) has to be climbed on the way from Tirano. There is an Italian proverb ('*Engiadina, terra fina, se non fosse la pruina*') to the effect that the Engadine is a fine place but for the frost. But visitors have always been prepared to put up with the frost—which can add piquancy when an otherwise warm summer evening is followed by a layer of hoarfrost in the morning.

The year 1760, an important date in European history, which saw the first publication of the *Nouvelle Héloise*, marks a turning point in Switzerland's relationship with the rest of Europe. The Treaty of Paris, signed in that year, brought the Seven Years War to an end, and Europe was now open to exploration by peaceful travellers. What had previously been individual exploits, with all their attendant perils, now became more peaceful, civilised journeys by accepted routes.

The new-found impetus to travel abroad and to visit places till then unseen, and probably unheard of, coincided with and, to some extent, inspired the Romantic Revival which gathered strength towards the end of the century. From now on, the pre-eminence of classical order, and a highly urbanised form of society, gave way to a passion for all things Gothic and the wildest, most melodramatic scenery. Rousseau provided much of the original theoretical work and emphasised the contrast between man in his original state of nature and man corrupted by the evil influences of civilisation. The ideal man to Rousseau was a mountain peasant, and this new enthusiasm could be most easily illustrated in the Swiss mountains.

The poet William Wordsworth, more closely associated than

anyone else with the Romantic movement in England, paid several visits to the Alps from 1790 onwards and, though primarily concerned with his political reactions to the invasion of Switzerland by the French revolutionary armies, he remained a poet of the mountains. His sister Dorothy also contributed much that was felicitous to Alpine literature, and her description of the approach to Grindelwald, greatly admired by Sir Arnold Lunn, shows the kind of inspiration which Switzerland now provided:

> Soon the vale lay before us with its two glaciers, and as it might seem, its *thousand* cabins sown upon the steeps. The descent became so precipitous that all were obliged to walk: deep we go into the broad cradle valley; every cottage we passed had its small garden, and cherry-trees sprinkled with leaves, bearing half-grown, half-ripe fruit. In plunging into this vale I was overcome with a sense of melancholy pervading the whole scene—not desolation, or dreariness: it is not the melancholy of the Scotch Highlands; but connected with social life in loneliness, not less than with the strife of all the seasons. When near the bottom of the declivity we were almost stunned by the roaring of the stream—under our feet (as it seemed); and from the centre of the wooden bridge, we beheld it issuing from its icy cavern beneath the snow-like roof of the larger Glacier. A cold blast, following the river, blew upon us while we passed over the bridge. I shall never forget the wintry sensation. The blast seemed as if its birth-place was in the icy cavern, and thence issuing, it would be fed with indestructible power.

Shelley, who was seldom influenced by any place for long, was equally impressed:

> Range after range of black mountains are seen extending one before the other, and far behind all, towering above every feature of the scene, the snowy Alps. They were a

hundred miles distant, but reach so high in the heavens that they look like those accumulated clouds of dazzling white that arrange themselves on the horizon during summer. Their immensity staggers the imagination, and so far surpasses all conception, that it requires an effort of imagination to believe that they indeed form a part of the earth.

By now the temporary interruption in the growth of European travel caused by the Napoleonic wars was coming to an end, and the real English invasion was at hand. It developed with incredible rapidity from now until the end of the nineteenth century. John Ruskin, who had more effect on Victorian society than any comparable writer could hope to attain nowadays, did a great deal to encourage enthusiasm for Switzerland and the Alps. His first visit dated from 1833. He was to live until 1900, and for most of the rest of his life he was obsessed by his own highly individual form of mountain philosophy. An objective balance could scarcely be expected of Ruskin, and in time he steeped himself so much in the virtues he found in the high hills that he began to regard visits by others as an intrusion. He feared the 'consuming white leprosy of new hotels and perfumers' shops', although Switzerland must have a better reputation than any country in Europe for the good taste with which it has controlled building development. He also attacked that highly esteemed body the Alpine Club in his contemptuous diatribe:

> The Alps themselves, which your own poets used to love so reverently, you look upon as soaped poles in a beargarden, which you set yourselves to climb and slide down again with 'shrieks of delight'.

It is slightly ironic that the members of the club were sufficiently compassionate, or perhaps cunning, to persuade him to become a member shortly thereafter.

From now on the English influence was paramount—with the Scots making their own contribution by persuading the Swiss to start curling. As will be seen, the English were instrumental in starting the Cresta run, and the bob run which grew out of it; we brought a peculiar form of ice-hockey (called bandy) to Switzerland; we were much concerned with the introduction of ski-ing to Switzerland, and certainly the organisation of ski-ing as a competitive sport was almost entirely due to the efforts of a few Englishmen, in particular Sir Arnold Lunn, who invented the slalom form of race.

It was, however, mountaineering which brought the most athletic visitors to Switzerland long before the winter sports season had started. Experts claim that the golden age of mountaineering began in 1854 when two Englishmen, Blackwell and Wells, made the first ascent of the Wetterhorn, and this period of high adventure lasted until Charles Hudson and the great Edward Whymper finally climbed the Matterhorn in 1865. To pursue the traditional classification, mountaineering's silver age, dominated throughout by Mummery, lasted until 1882 when the Dent du Géant was conquered by W. W. Graham and, the only non-Englishman involved in these records, Sella of Italy. The English were not, of course, the only mountaineers, and most of the ascents were made in partnership with local guides; but the enthusiasm, the determination and eventually many of the more scientific skills all came from the English. It was under English auspices, too, that the Alpine Club was formed in 1857, and from then on mountaineering had some claims to be recognised as an organised sport. The membership of the club in its earlier years showed clearly what exhilaration and recreation the more responsible Victorians found on the face of the Alpine peaks. The records demonstrate that the members were almost entirely churchmen, or those who had done the State some service, or were distinguished in the law, or who were escaping from the more mundane and constricting pursuits of the City. Mountaineering was regarded as the ideal antidote to materialism.

The winter season was to follow soon after, and its development at St Moritz, started by Badrutt's famous bet in 1864, is described in the next chapter. Skating was for many years supreme; the Cresta and the toboggan were the next on the scene; bandy was popular; but a remarkably long period was to elapse before ski-ing obtained a strong hold on winter visitors. As late as 1903, skiers at St Moritz were referred to contemptously as 'plank-hoppers'.

Before then, however, a surprising manifestation was to take place: the sudden growth of the great English travel agencies. Three of the pioneer agencies all had respectable roots in Victorian philosophy. They were Christian by origin, and they were intent on improving the lot of others. They had a religious background. Sir Henry Lunn, the prime mover in Swiss terms, was a Reunionist; the Polytechnic emerged from the religious and philanthropic activities of the then Mr Quintin Hogg; and Thomas Cook, the travel organiser supreme, had first put his ability to use in Sunday-school activities.

Lunn was a highly individual character and in his son's words he first came to notice when he 'patented an invention for attaching scoring dials to tennis rackets'. After promoting religious gatherings of his fellow Reunionists, Lunn was the first agent to see that the Alpine regions in winter were much in need of some form of organisation to promote tourist traffic. This he developed in a very personal way by offering special terms to Etonians and Harrovians at Adelboden. Thereafter it was a short step to forming the Public Schools Alpine Sports Club. This unusual body dominated the winter sports scene throughout the Alps. It operated a considerable number of centres, including Champfer near St Moritz, but not St Moritz itself. In these centres the club had a priority and in some cases a monopoly of hotel reservations. It was not only a case of snow white forming an agreeable background to old school colours, there was even the macabre sight of visitors from other countries being denied lodging because they were not members of the PSASC. Sir Henry Lunn, whose standing in the Swiss world was such that he could refer to himself as 'the Prime Minister of Murren', saw the club develop

far further than he can ever have expected, despite his un-
doubted genius for organisation. The club was eventually killed
by the financial crisis in 1931.

Before leaving the wider aspects of holidays in Switzerland
for the more particular scene at St Moritz it is worth recalling
the description by Sir Henry Lunn's son, Arnold, of a winter
season at Adelboden in 1902, which has an unmistakable period
flavour. Guests at the Grand Hotel dined at two long tables:

> We danced three or four times a week, and devoted the
> remaining evenings to indoor gymkhanas and amateur
> theatricals. The polka and the lancers were just dying out
> and it was still considered rather fast to reverse.

2

Pioneers

The Alps have always attracted their fair share of travellers,
sometimes very intrepid ones, who have made their way over
the passes of Switzerland and, what interests us most, to the
Grisons and the Engadine Valley. The reactions of early
visitors were very different from what ours would be today.
They were less inspired by the melodramatic aspects of the
scenery—all that absurd glamour, as D. H. Lawrence called
it. He added that he hated the 'stark and shroudy whiteness'.
There was little social and even less sporting life to attract
them and the only preoccupations of the first foreigners to
break into the happy valley of the Inn which have survived are
their enthusiasm for Alpine flora and for the curative properties
of the local waters.

Sir Gavin de Beer, in his authoritative account of *Early
Travellers in the Alps*, emphasises that the first phase of Alpine
travel ended at about the close of the eighteenth century. Thereafter the repercussions of the French Revolution discouraged
travel for some time to come, and when it was resumed more
modern developments produced an entirely new atmosphere:
we were in the age of *il gran turismo*.

St Moritz's first recorded admirer—as opposed to folklore
and local tradition—was the sixteenth-century physician Paracelsus or, to give him his full name, Philip Aureolus Theo-
phrastus Bombastus von Hohenheim, who described the local
springs in glowing terms. But his affection for the area was not
shared by two contemporary French poets—Joachim Du Bellay

and Olivier de Magny—who both visited the Grisons about
1557. In Sir Gavin de Beer's racy translation Du Bellay said that
anyone who like Oedipus had killed his father, or like Orestes
caused his mother's death, in order to expiate his abominable
crimes,

> Let him just journey through the Grisons,
> That is, if he wants rebate of God's grace.

De Magny was no more favourably disposed,

> Rather would I endure a heavy storm at sea,
> Thirty days on end, in danger of shipwreck
> Provided that this danger did not materialise,
> Than cross the Grisons, Aprica and Bernina passes,
> The bridge of Camogasc and the pont Arrasine,
> With their infamous stoves and inhabitants.

Early visitors to the area included Sir Edward Unton in 1563,
but it is not clear from his servant's diary, which has miracu-
lously survived, how far he penetrated into the Engadine. Next
came Fynes Moryson, who travelled through the Grisons in
1595. He came over the Bernina Pass and eventually made his
way over the Albula to Lenzerheide. That indefatigable and
ubiquitous pilgrim Thomas Coryat—Shakespeare's Autolycus
come to life—also visited the Alps in 1608 and characteristically
felt entitled to confer on himself the sobriquet *montiscandentis-
simus*. The title of his work refers specifically to the Grisons:
'Coryat's Crudities hastily gobled up in five moneths Travells
in France, Savoy, Italy, Rhetia, comonly called the Gryson's
country; Helvetia alias Switzerland, some parts of High
Germany, and the Netherlands; newly digested in the hungry
air of Odcombe in the County of Somerset, and now dispersed
to the nourishment of Travelling Members of this Kingdome.'
Coryat asks: 'What, I pray you, is more pleasant, more delect-
able, and more acceptable unto a man than to behold the height
of hills, as it were the very Atlantes themselves of heaven?'

An important visitor at the beginning of the eighteenth

century was Johann Jakob Scheuchzer of Zürich, a Fellow of
the Royal Society of London to whom he dedicated his *Itinera
Alpina*. A renowned natural scientist, he was also a professional
tourist and undertook nine Alpine expeditions from 1702 to 1711,
invariably studying the effect of height on his barometer. It was
on his second journey in 1703 that he visited the baths at St
Moritz and returned by Champfer and the Julier Pass. (Sir
Gavin de Beer observes that the original name of Champfer was
Campo di Ferro and refers to the remarkable hardness of the
ground 'which could scarcely be dug with any instruments'.)
Scheuchzer was disappointed not to find on the pillars at the
top of the Julier Pass the inscriptions '*Hucusque non ultra*' and
'*Omitto Rhetos indomitos*' which had been mentioned by pre-
vious travellers, but a print of the columns is reproduced in his
Natural History of Switzerland.

Alpine travel was still thought to be full of danger when
Johann Gesner wrote in 1726 that he 'had indeed intended to
push on from Hinterrhein to the St Gotthard, but there was no
way which would not strike terror into my then young mind'.
Throughout the eighteenth century, however, the volume of
Alpine literature grew steadily and there was no more distinguished visitor than Archdeacon William Coxe, who made
several expeditions from 1776 to 1786. In Switzerland he felt
that he was 'breathing the air of liberty; every person here has
apparently the mien of content and satisfaction'. In 1779 he
arrived at the Grisons by way of Chiavenna and came to the
Engadine over the Maloja Pass. The Engadine was much to his
liking and the spirit of neatness he found so general that he
scarcely observed 'one bad house through the whole district'.
The Archdeacon must, however, have been disappointed that
the religious tolerance which earlier visitors to the Grisons had
noted with surprise and satisfaction—churches being sometimes shared by Protestant and Catholic congregations—was
now somewhat in decline. (Five years earlier Carlo Anton Pilati
di Tassullo related that at St Moritz there was now a fine of one
hundred crowns for saying mass, even in private rooms.)

Kaſpar   Annetta   Maria Tognoni-Badrutt   Johannes Badrutt-Berry   Johannes   Peter Robert

Alfons   Roſina Rocco-Badrutt/Sidogna   Maria Badrutt-Berry   Paul
    Urſula Tognoni-Badrutt

The progenitor: Johannes Badrutt *en famille*

Hurrying to the slopes, 1883

Early Cresta: Grand National competitors, 1891

Husbands in harness, 1895

An early curling match, 1900

A mixed bob team, 1904

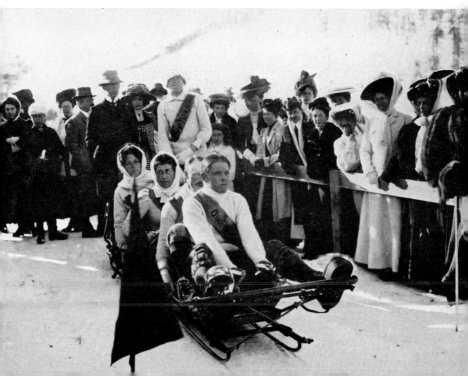

The first ski-kijöring race, 1906

Timing the Cresta, 1908

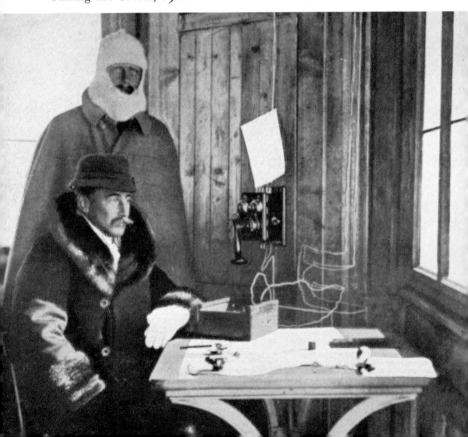

The St Moritz Curling Club: rink and clubhouse

A youthful Gordon Richards watched by Billy Griggs

Straight on the broom

Never too early to start

Butterflies in the stomach?

Through the gate

Gathering speed

The clubhouse at Junction

There were booms in European travel after each European war—the Seven Years War, the wars of the French Revolution in 1802 and the Napoleonic wars in 1814 and 1815. On each occasion peace brought a quickening of desire for foreign travel and the numbers grew. The year 1870 is taken to mark a turning point in Swiss tourism. It saw both the highest peaks so far in tourist development—and another interruption caused by the start of the Franco-Prussian War. Three years earlier an Englishman, Walter M. Moore, laid claim 'to the honour of being the first English Traveller who ever spent a winter in the Engadine. I say the first "traveller", because one Englishman (Mr Strettell) had certainly been there before me, but as he lived there and had built a house at St Moritz, I consider him more as a resident than a visitor.'

In 1870 an expedition to St Moritz still had its own perils on the journey and uncertainty on arrival. The village itself aroused fairly pungent criticism from the more delicately bred visitors—whose objectives then would be taking the cure, or mountaineering, or botany, for St Moritz was still primarily a summer resort. The Engadine was described in *Thomas Cook's Tourist Handbook* of the time as 'producing in abundance grain and wild flowers. *Voilà tout!* Its dry, clear atmosphere and intensely blue skies are proverbial, and it is hemmed in by majestic mountains and glacial scenery. For sketchers, botanists, butterfly-collectors, Alpine climbers and others, the Engadine is a very paradise.'

The intrepid voyager would leave London at 7.45 am and by Dover and Calais would reach Paris at six o'clock the same evening. He would then board the Swiss express and, leaving at 8.05 pm, would arrive at Basle at nine o'clock the next morning in time for breakfast (no meals were served on the trains and resort to the station buffet was necessary: the nostalgic smell of new-baked bread, cherry jam, Swiss coffee and kirsch) and the 10.30 am train for Chur. If there was time available, diversions could be made at Zürich, crossing the lake to Rapperswil by steamer, and at Ragaz to visit the famous

c

Pfäffers gorge, but in any event the now wearied traveller would reach Chur at 7 pm, thirty-six hours after leaving London. An overnight stop would be recommended.

Chur—the old part of the town has changed little in the last century—was, improbably, a great favourite of Thackeray's. In his *Roundabout Papers* he recalled with enthusiasm that he had 'seldom seen a place more quaint, pretty, calm, and pastoral than this remote little Chur. What need have the inhabitants for walls and ramparts, except to build summerhouses, to trail vines, and hang clothes to dry? No enemies approach the great mouldering gate; only at morn and even the cows come lowing past them, the village maidens chatter merrily round the fountain, and babble like the ever-voluble stream that flows under the walls. The schoolboys, with book and satchel, in smart uniforms, march up to the Gymnasium, and return thence at their stated time'—an idyllic view which lacks Thackeray's normal astringency. It must be admitted that Chur also suffers from suffocatingly severe snowstorms in winter and torrential rain in the summer—when the swollen Rhine provokes little lyrical rapture.

A day's march from Chur by diligence would finish the journey to St Moritz. A start was made at 5 am: tempers were not at their best after an interrupted semi-Alpine slumber and there was much jostling for seats. Wise virgins had sent telegrams in advance to reserve seats in the diligence. Foolish ones were at the mercy of the stagecoach employees, a notably peremptory race, and might be interred in the diligence or placed uncomfortably in some ancillary vehicle. The charge for an inside place from Chur to St Moritz was 14s. 9d.

After Chur there are two possible routes from Tiefencastel— by the Albula to Samaden, three miles from St Moritz, or over the Julier Pass to Silvaplana and St Moritz from the west. A nineteenth-century doctor, James Yeo, who published a professionally clinical account of the curative powers of the local springs in *A Season at St Moritz* recalls how M. Michelet used to select routes on the grounds that '*je préfère les grandes voies historiques où l'humanité a passé'*. This would mean the Julier. The Romans used it, and before them the Rhaetian province was inhabited by an early Celtic population. There is no convincing philological or historical proof that the pass is named after either Julius Caesar or one of the Celtic gods 'Jul', but it seems certain that medieval pilgrims, merchants and others on their way to the Crusades climbed its heights on their journey to Venice and the East. Only Hannibal seems to have preferred another route over the Alps.

After a stop for refreshments at Mühlen there remained the two-hour climb from Bivio to the summit of the Julier. The pass has been described as 'a scene of mixed grandeur and desolation. The most perfect silence and stillness prevailed on every side, broken only by the cracking of the whips of the postboys. No tree, no blade of grass, nothing but huge stones, hurled down from the decaying mountains around, with here and there a patch of snow.' The summit lies on a ridge between two peaks, the Piz Munteratsch and the Pulashin, and at the top of the pass there is a small lake and two granite pillars—erected, according to choice, by Julius Caesar or the Celts. Theodore Andrea Cook later (in 1894), describing the Cresta run, reflected that 'the stone pillars surely marked the starting point of one of the longest toboggan runs before or since; and I cannot resist believing that the great commander, fertile in resources, there first showed his troops the way to use their shields and spears as instruments of locomotion'. It would be interesting, but unwise, to accept this as the origin of tobogganing and ski-ing.

Once through the pillars there followed a rapid descent to the meadows and lakes of Silvaplana—a sharp contrast to the splendid isolation of the pass—a quarter of an hour to Champfer and only three more miles to St Moritz. But it was not all edelweiss and glühwein when the steaming horses were reined in at the Kurhaus. Pressure on tourist accommodation is not a twentieth-century phenomenon and Dr Yeo remembered ruefully that he had been warned in London, in Paris, at Basle, at

Zürich, at Chur, and indeed at every stopping place on the road that St Mortiz was full, full to overflowing. And so it proved. He describes the alarming confusion and disappointment at the Bureau de Poste. 'Unprotected females in ones and twos, as well as in larger and in formidable groups, were making violent and as it seemed unsuccessful attempts to force an entrance into the chief hotel of the place; others were wandering about in a state of disconsolate uncertainty.' And who could challenge his conclusion that 'nervous ladies, in delicate health, arriving at St Moritz on an August evening, with a keen wind blowing along the valley, and something suspiciously like snow in the air (and such evenings do occasionally occur in the Upper Engadine, even in August) are not likely to be benefited by even a temporary residence in something little better than a barn?' Not surprisingly Dr Yeo contrasts this with the frugal but sufficient fare (apart from the toughness of the beef), the excellent breakfast and the unsurpassed coffee which he found at the Engadine Kulm Hotel.

While recognising the great scenic attraction of the area—admitted even by the caustic *Edinburgh Review*—Dr Yeo found much to complain of at St Moritz. The village he thought untidy, badly built and badly drained, and there was no proper provision for Anglican Church services—then held in the Kurhaus in the morning and in the Protestant village church in the evening. At the Kurhaus the occasional hurried entrance of a waiter forgetful that the *salon de danse* of the night before was an English church on the following morning pointed to the need for a 'permanent and exclusively ecclesiastical edifice'. The village church had the 'most uncomfortable seats ever devised for the punishment of the devout and long-suffering Protestant —good old Puritan seats, especially designed for mortifying the flesh'.

Dr Yeo's main concern was the 'cure', which during the latter part of last century afforded the real magnet to attract visitors to St Moritz. The cure had a respectable ancestry. The Romans used the St Moritz springs and in 1519 Pope Leo X is said to have issued an edict granting indulgence to pilgrims who visited the shrine of St Mauritius. The earliest written account (1537) comes from Paracelsus, who described their beneficial effect. He wrote: 'Of all the mineral springs in Europe known to me, I give preference to that which I found at St Moritz, the water of which is in August as acid as vinegar. He who takes this water medicinally regains his health, and will never be troubled by stone or gravel, gout or arthritis. It strengthens the stomach so that it can digest tartar even as an ostrich digests iron and a blackbird sand. And not only tartar but everything else in food and drink which might bring about a disorder.'

The Swiss never look a gift horse in the mouth and Paracelsus has accordingly been adopted by St Moritz, publicly revered and given a place of honour ever since—the principal well is named after him. From 1680 the waters were exported for consumption elsewhere and German, Italian and Swiss visitors started appearing at the springs from 1700 onwards. But there was no unanimity about the excellence of the early springs. In 1703 Johann Jakob Scheuchzer described them as tasting almost like ink, and half a century later Gabriel Walser said that the water at St Moritz 'acts violently, makes one quite silly in the head and takes one's strength away; indeed, for the first few days one feels so slack and tired that one can scarcely cross the road'. Nor was the accommodation for addicts of the springs up to later Swiss standards. A German visitor, J. F. Heigelin, in 1790 complained that 'Although the [St Moritz] spring has been provided with a little house and thereby brought under cover, we found everything wretched and falling to pieces; not even the slightest comforts for cure-guests, and, except for the narrow and marshy valley of the Inn, the well-stocked lake and the beautiful road to Samaden and Zuoz, nothing to entertain and distract a stranger.'

The situation had not apparently improved in the next thirty years, for Karl Kasthofer found that 'The spring, which is situated at a quarter of a league from the nearest house, flows into a sort of vault or reservoir, which has, quite wrongly, been

given the pompous name of salle: it is there that the drinkers
sit. The ground between the village and the spring is partly
marshy, and the path leading to it is badly kept. It is therefore
to be presumed that the invalids who visit the spring, exposed
as they are to the inclemencies of the weather on the way to it,
and to inevitable chills on the spot, must often purchase relief
from their old sufferings at the cost of new complaints.' And in
1841 a French visitor, Rodolphe Töpffer, gives a marvellously
evocative picture of the resort of this time: St Moritz is described as 'a little town composed of stables and billiard-saloons
where bearded bath-guests pass their time; one of those places
that owe to the transient presence of invalids a little false
vivacity, much cigar smoke, and a grotesque mixture of busy
peasants, idle gentry, tipplers, makers of cheese, and of cannons
at billiards.'

A remarkable example of early craftsmanship was detected
in 1852 when during reconstruction work on the spring it was
found that what 'was evidently the ancient conduit of the
mineral source' consisted of a huge trunk hollowed out from a
larch tree. It was not, however, till 1857 that an itinerant
English clergyman—and what would the Continent be without
the discoveries of these nomadic pastors?—detected the spring
at St Moritz and started its popularity with the English. Those
who took the cure drank the waters and bathed in them, and
the routine followed by suppliants at the two wells, the Alte
Quelle and the Paracelsus, was Spartan. From six o'clock in
the morning in the sharp air these hardy pilgrims could be seen
pacing round the Kurhaus to the melancholy strains of the
sleepy minstrels who provided the 'Kurmusik'. The ration rose
from one to six glasses daily with a half-hour's march inter-
vening—purification by survival.

After breakfast, baths—a course of twenty-five—were obligatory. The baths were long, narrow wooden boxes and 'an
unusually stout and tall man would find himself straitened for
room in one'. Each box was covered by a lid fitting round the
neck of the inmate, giving the effect, as Dr Yeo observes, of a

modified pillory. Apoplectic patients soon assumed a gargoyle-
like appearance as they gasped for air. Such were the rigours
that the seekers after health would endure. An English visitor,
William Marcet, in 1858 had tried 'how long I could remain in
the water; after about twenty-five minutes, commencing to feel
uncomfortable, I got out of the bath, but was so intoxicated and
tottering from the effects of the carbonic acid, that I could
hardly dress. I rushed out into the fresh air, but just able to
stand.' But while there was still some medical dispute about the
therapeutic value of the St Moritz springs when applied exter-
nally, by now there was none about their palatable flavour.
They had a strong carbonic acid content and a markedly
chalybeate taste. The author of *The Regular Swiss Round* found
them 'delicious—far too nice for medicine, though they are said
to perform great cures. They combine the finest flavour of the
best soda and seltzer water, iced. There is a keen, refreshing
edge to them which spreads all over your being, and sharpens
you up at once.' This was an eloquent advertisement—enough
to outweigh the not very luxurious accommodation in the
Kurhaus, which was never popular with the English, who much
preferred Badrutt's Kulm Hotel. It is all more scientific and
more comfortable nowadays.

But winter guests were also beginning to appear. The origin
of St Moritz's winter season derives from the wager between
four Englishmen and Johannes Badrutt, the owner of the
Kulm Hotel. The scene of this historic event, which took
place on an autumn evening in 1864, was set round the log fire
in the Engadine lounge of the Kulm. Four Englishmen were
finishing their summer holiday and, as was their custom, were
spending their last evening in relaxed discourse with their host
Johannes Badrutt. It seems as though Archdeacon Coxe might
really have had Badrutt in mind when he wrote that his host
was 'an open-hearted, honest Swiss: he brings his pint of wine,
sits down to table with us, and chats without the least ceremony.
There is a certain forwardness of this kind which is insupport-
able when it apparently is the effect of impertinent curiosity, or

fawning officiousness; but the present instance of frank fami-
liarity, arising from a mind conscious of its natural equality, and
unconstrained by arbitrary distinction, is highly pleasing; as the
demeanour of unsophisticated nature is far preferable to the
false refinements of artificial manners.' The Swiss hotelier had
enjoyed a successful season and was happy to provide an extra
measure or two of kirsch from his cellars in the rocks. So far
this had been a farewell evening—like many before and since—
but it proved to be one of quite unexpected significance for the
entire Engadine.

The fire was down to the embers and the guests were rising
reluctantly from their seats when Badrutt, in halting English,
stated his proposition: 'The warm summer is over, autumn
has crept into the valley and winter stands at the door. But, do
you know that the winter up here is more pleasant and less cold
than it is in London? Do you know that during the hours of
sunshine—and in St Moritz the sun is hardly ever hidden—
you can stroll around without an overcoat or hat, and even
without a jacket, whereas if you did that in London the result
would be pneumonia?'

His guests did not at first take him seriously. The mountains
in the summer months were all very well, but the winter was
another matter. They knew what it was like in London when,
with the first flurry of snow, everyone started to shiver and
wait impatiently for it to clear. It would be madness to spend
time and energy on the long journey to St Moritz only to shiver
even more and with no hope of the snow clearing.

Mr Badrutt, however, was not joking. He thought quickly
over the good results of the summer: 'I offer you,' he said, 'the
opportunity of verifying my assertions personally. You will be
my guests for the whole of next winter and I will accommodate
you, free of charge, at the Kulm Hotel. Will you accept my
offer? Let's make it a bet!'

The English visitors thought this was a fair wager: they took
it on. The agreement was that, towards Christmas, they would
come to St Moritz for a trial holiday. If it transpired that

Johannes Badrutt's predictions were wrong, he would pay all their travelling expenses from London to St Moritz and return. If, however, he proved to be right, he would welcome them as his guests until the spring. It seemed to the Englishmen that they could lose nothing—except a few months spent in less salubrious weather conditions than a London winter. The Engadiner, on the other hand, felt that he was most unlikely to lose. He knew his friends well enough to be sure that they would pay for some of the contents of his cellar and that there was a strong possibility that they would bring with them paying members of their families. He knew too, as they did not, that the much lower temperatures at St Moritz as compared to London were offset by the extreme dryness of the air and by the hours of sunshine—something that London could not boast. In his imagination he could see his hotel in the future with a full complement of guests in the winter as well as the summer.

Towards Christmas the Englishmen set off for Switzerland with members of their families. Their older relatives stayed behind, being of the opinion that anyone who attempted to go to the mountains in winter must suffer from some mental aberration. The valiant four were beginning to regret the whole undertaking: but a bet is a bet. And anyhow they would have the satisfaction of putting something across the predatory Badrutt and could be home again shortly after the New Year.

They hired a sleigh at Chur to take them to Lenzerheide and over the Julier to St Moritz and wrapped themselves in furs. A special sleigh was necessary to transport their huge mound of luggage. In spite of their meticulous preparations, they forgot one essential thing—sunglasses. The Julier was bathed in sunshine and, instead of reaching their destination in the frozen condition they had expected, they arrived perspiring and half blinded by the sunlight on the snow. In place of the dark mountain winter they had expected, the light was pitilessly brilliant and far more intense than in summer.

At the entrance of his hotel stood Badrutt in his shirt-sleeves, the bristles on his beard curling triumphantly. He had already won his bet. As promised, his guests stayed with him till Easter. His generosity was well rewarded. At the first melting of the snow the Englishmen returned to London, suntanned, bursting with health and the joy of living and enthusiastic about the winter season in the mountains. The following winter they went back again, but this time as paying guests and accompanied by many friends. The popularity of Swiss winter holidays was established and from the very start the English were the most frequent and popular visitors.

Unfortunately the tale—which is preserved as St Moritz's favourite legend—is incomplete, since the names of the guests can not now be identified. The Badrutt records, however, show that the following guests arrived at the Kulm in the winter of 1864–5:

J. D. Walker, Univ. Coll.	England
Douglas W. Freshfield, Univ. Coll.	England
R. Beachoroff, Univ. Coll.	England
H. A. Boyle	England
C. P. Knight	England
Dr Watson	London
Miss Watson	London
Mr Arthur Watson	London
R. Ramsden, Trin. Coll.	Cambridge
F. H. Scott, Trin. Coll.	Cambridge
J. S. Edgecombe	London
J. Edward White	London
Thos. Starling Simson	London
Shrewsbury	London
Rev. R. S. and Miss Hunt, Univ. Coll.	England

Another entry in the visitors' book confirms that Badrutt was really betting on a certainty:

We spent $5\frac{1}{2}$ months at Herr Badrutt's and feel ourselves much indebted to the great kindness of himself, his wife and the whole family. They made our winter quarters so comfortable, that we were loathe to leave them when spring came. Any doubts we had entertained as to the possibility of keeping warm indoors, in a locality where in the open air the temperature was often below zero Fahrenheit in the shade, were speedily dispelled owing to the extreme dryness of the air; we never found our sitting-room comfortable above 56° Fahrt. a temperature that would be unbearable in winter in the more humid climate of England. The rooms are warmed by means of stoves,—not open fireplaces—consequently the chief difficulty is to ventilate them; to do this effectually we left our sitting-room for five minutes every two hours opening all the doors and windows. A pan of water kept in the stove is also indispensable to prevent the already dry air of St Moritz becoming overdried. On an average we were out four hours daily, walking, skating on the lakes, sleighing or sitting on the terrace reading, this latter two or three hours at a time. Twice in January we dined on the terrace and on other days had picnics in our sledges. Far from finding it cold, the heat of the sun is so intense at times that sun-shades were indispensable. The brilliancy of the sun, the blueness of the sky and the clearness of the atmosphere quite surprised us. The lake affords the opportunity to those who love the art of skating, without interruption for five months. The ice has to a certain extent to be artificially maintained. To do this we with other English friends formed a small club, first to keeping a circle clear of snow, secondly for renewing the surface whenever it became impaired, by turning a stream on to it. I must state, having spent part of the winter of 1863/64 at Mentone, I derived far more benefit from that of 1864/65 spent at St Moritz. The change from England to Mentone did me good at first; but latterly I experienced great lassitude; whilst at St Moritz I was far stronger at the end of the winter than at the commencement.

A pleasing picture, to support a letter which appeared in *The Times* of 21st February 1870, signed by the President of the St Moritz Skating Club. Skating at St Moritz seems to have started much earlier than the first concerted attempts to promote it there in 1882, for the President described how a suitable surface had been created on part of the St Moritz Lake by diverting a stream on to it by means of a sluice-gate and guiding chutes. The skating-grounds were first marked out with a low ridge of ice made from wet snow. In a few minutes the stream covered the ice on the chosen area and the stream was then returned to its own channel to run as before, under the ice into the lake. (In essence this is not very unlike the more sophisticated methods still in use.)

The President went on to enthuse over the delights of a season lasting from October to April and of skating under a brilliantly blue summer sky. He added that another favourite entertainment of the English as well as the natives was 'sliding down steep inclines on small sledges constructed for this purpose. The speed attainable is almost incredible.' Here too coming events were casting their Alpine shadows before.

The distinguished English essayist Sir Leslie Stephen, in his *The Playground of Europe* published in 1871, described a visit to St Moritz some two years earlier. His wife had been ordered to take the baths and, like Dr Yeo, he found much to criticise. 'We found in one hotel a King, an imperial duchess, and some other equal swells. . . . We should have had to pay like princes and lodge like pigs.' He went on in a strange optative way: 'I should rejoice if it could be made into the Norfolk Island of the Alps, and all kings, cockneys, persons travelling with couriers, Americans doing Europe against time, Cook's tourists and their like, commercial travellers, and especially that variety of English clergyman which travels in dazzling white ties and forces church services upon you by violence in remote country inns, could be confined within it to amuse or annoy each other.' With the temporary and understandable spleen distilled from it, there remains a striking picture of what St Moritz was going to look like at the next watershed in its history—1914. Before then, however, there was to be a further temporary interruption in its placid progress. A visitor to the town in 1870 describes succinctly the departure of the captains and kings at the outbreak of the Franco-Prussian War. 'At Bad St Moritz we were more than welcome. The Queen of Württemberg, the Grand Duchess of Baden, and all their suites, had left within the last forty-eight hours, recalled by telegraph to Germany. The war had already made pacific vacancies in the crowded ranks of the St Moritz bathers.' But they would soon come back.

3

Before the Howitzers

The rise in the number of visitors was not to be denied. The Engadine had been discovered as a new playground and, even during the melancholy hostilities between France and Prussia, St Moritz became yearly more populous. At nearby Davos, progress was almost arithmetical. W. G. and Margaret Lockett in *The Development of Winter Sports in the Engadine* noted that in the 1865–6 winter there were but two lonely visitors: in the next four years the numbers multiplied from twelve to twenty-five to fifty to seventy, and in the 1870–1 season, despite the outbreak of the war, there were ninety visitors.

During the period from 1870 to 1914 St Moritz changed its face from a hamlet to a resort de luxe. New hotels were built year after year as European society flocked over the Julier or up from Celerina; the winter season began to emulate the summer holidays; and most of the names in the visitors' register were English. Dr Tucker Wise, writing in 1885, had said that there were only two hotels open to receive those who wintered at St Moritz. As amenities, he could find only two ice-rinks in constant use and several tracks kept in good order for coasting and tobogganing. This seems to have been an underestimate, since the first English newspaper printed in Switzerland, which started its long career with a first edition on 7th September 1886, showed not two, but four, hotels in the village. The newspaper, which for long published a weekly list of amusements, events and visitors at St Moritz and Davos, listed the Kulm,

46

the Hotel Caspar Badrutt, the Hotel Beau-Rivage and the Privat-Hotel as being open, and by the end of January 1887 there were 240 visitors, nearly all British, in the four hotels. (The local paper, published in the Romansch language, *Il Fogl Ladin*, claimed 'the unheard of number of 450 visitors' some time earlier, but whatever the actual figure it is clear that the snowball had started to roll.)

St Moritz has since changed more than any of the other early Swiss resorts. While some of the original buildings are still preserved, it is much more difficult to visualise the appearance of St Moritz in the 1870s than it is to imagine what some of its sister resorts were like then. There are three aspects of St Moritz's progress up to the First World War which force themselves on attention. First, the changes which took place were not incidental: they were not caused by outside events, apart from expectations that the number of foreign visitors would increase; they were devised by an unusually far-seeing and imaginative group of local hoteliers. The Badrutt family, who for long dominated the scene, soon to be followed by the Bons who built Suvretta House, and the many other inspired men who have since been in charge of individual enterprises and of the Kurverein, have contrived to keep St Moritz in the very forefront of the international scene. It is no accident that *The Times* in London never fails to publish details of the hours of sunshine, the temperature, and the depth of the snowfall during the winter season and even records the performance and times during practice runs on the Cresta and bobsleigh runs. St Moritz's international reputation is due to the foresight of those who laid the foundations at the end of last century and the determination of those who have since ensured that it can still claim to be the premier resort of the Engadine.

But the actual patterns of this rapid development did not all originate in the Engadine Valley, and the proportion of English visitors was so substantial that Anglo-Saxon influence on the shape which the new projects took was very pronounced. Squire Bancroft observed that in winter the life very much resembles that on shipboard—for, unlike the summer season, people do not now merely come and go—so in a short while everyone seems to know everybody else.

Dame Katherine Furse, the daughter of John Addington Symonds, a pioneer of British ski-ing, quotes from a letter written by her mother from the Engadiner Kulm on 17th February 1884:

> Johnnie and I with Lotta have come over to the Engadine for a few days' visit on the occasion of a tobogganing race, and are having a very happy time. This Kulm Hotel is a most curious place and well worth a winter visit; it is *immense*, all built at odd times and in various bits, so that no two sets of rooms are alike—and there is a friendly hospitable *homey* feeling in the whole place which makes it feel like paying a visit to old friends in an English country house. I know nothing like it anywhere else. We have several old friends in the house—who have lived here many winters and a large colony besides—but all are alike in being kind to us visitors. It is most delightful.

This must have been halfway through the chaplaincy of the Rev. A. B. Strettell, who is commemorated by a brass plate in the Villa Grünenberg (above the Leaning Tower) for his thirty-eight years of service in the English church. Robert Browning was another frequent visitor:

> We have walked every day, morning and evening—after-noon, I should say—two or three hours each excursion, the delicious mountain air surpassing any I was ever privi-leged to breathe. My sister is absolutely herself again, and something over.

And three years later, 1887, he reflected that, although they were snowed up and could not leave their house to go to the hotel opposite where they got their meals:

(such is the Alpine treatment of travellers!) our amends is in the magnificence of the mountain, and its firs black against the universal white.

The Duchess of Teck said that she could never have got through all the work of Queen Victoria's Golden Jubilee 'without St Moritz's restoring power'. At the same time, that spirited memorialist Mrs Aubrey Le Blond found the prime aesthete Oscar Browning staying at St Moritz and

> knowing a certain little weakness of his, I had placed two comfortable basket chairs at the end of the tennis court with two large labels on them 'Reserved for T.R.Hs.' I also put a few smaller chairs next them. In one of those more modest chairs sat Oscar Browning for at least one hopeful hour, in fact till he discovered that our distinguished visitors had been installed for some time in the gallery above.

But to preserve the balance visitors were not all so fanciful. It was necessary to place in one of the dining-rooms the stern injunction 'Dogs will by all means be chased from public rooms', and to make it clear that 'To prevent disagreeableness and reclamation for luncheon and dinner *table d'hôte* visitors are highly requested to be there at the appointed time'.

The third interesting element in the annals of the village up to the time of the First World War is that, although winter sports grew more rapidly in St Moritz than anywhere else, it was never a centre for the first Alpine sport—mountaineering. It is true that Father Placidus a Specha, who has claims to be the first true mountaineer who climbed extensively for fun, was born in the Grisons in 1752, but the peaks round St Moritz, from Piz Nair in the north to Piz Corvatsch in the south, were not of a kind to attract the real mountaineering enthusiast. There is no record of St Moritz appealing to the great mountaineering names of Whymper, Mummery or Geoffrey Winthrop Young. Visitors came to St Moritz to practise various other

D

Alpine sports, even when they did not share the mountaineer's frenzy described by George Meredith:

> Carry your fever to the Alps, you of minds diseased: not to sit down in sight of them ruminating, for bodily ease and comfort will trick the soul and set you measuring our lean humanity against yonder sublime and infinite; but mount, rack the limbs, wrestle it out among the peaks; taste danger, sweat, earn rest: learn to discover ungrudgingly that haggard fatigue is the fair vision you have run to earth, and that rest is your uttermost reward. Would you know what it is to hope again, and have all your hopes at hand?—hang upon the crags at a gradient that makes your next stop a debate between the thing you are and the thing you may become.

Instead, from 1880 to the end of the century, St Moritz built the first toboggan run, the Cresta; and the bobsleigh, together with the first Bobsleigh Club in the world, appeared soon after. Ice skating and curling had both been known in the Swiss Alps long before, and the first European skating competition was held in the Grisons. There was much competition between the English and Swedish schools of figure skating, with the latter eventually prevailing. Curling, long famous in Scotland, also found its way to St Moritz, and the first game played on the Continent took place on Herr Badrutt's ice. Ice-hockey developed from 'bandy' (first played in the English Fens), and ski-joring was started on the frozen St Moritz Lake. Ski-ing has such an influence on the subsequent story that it is dealt with at legnth in later parts of this book. All in all, two decades saw St Moritz change from a watering place to a *station des sports d'hiver*, a description which it retains in the first rank.

Meanwhile, in 1904, a much-needed permanent link with the rest of Europe was provided by the long-awaited appearance of the railway. The Albula branch reached St Moritz in that year, later than elsewhere because of the extraordinary difficulties of construction, the building of spirals and viaducts, and the

exceptionally long Albula tunnel itself. The journey to St
Moritz could now be accomplished without incident, and the
stage was finally set. New hotels were still being built, and
development proceeded apace, but it was surely of J. V.
Widman, writing about Nietzsche, a regular Swiss visitor,
when he said:

> Who knows but that his bitterest and most anti-human
> expression, that of the 'Many too many', may not have been
> provoked by the sight of the tourists who in swarms over-
> run the Engadine every summer?

Admittedly, Theodore Andrea Cook, an early Secretary of the
St Moritz Tobogganing Club, had already confessed that
'perhaps the best friends of St Moritz are those who spread its
fame the least', but surely he was speaking with his tongue in
his cheek.

Some of the exotic pastimes which appeared, and disappeared after a short time, must have astounded the native
population. In the 1890s regular cricket matches were played
between teams representing St Moritz and Maloja, where a
club was formed in 1895. The reactions of the Engadiners to
this (or to the formation, about the same time, of the Anglo-
American Baseball Club) have not been recorded. The disciples
of Montgolfier came hard on the heels of the cricketers; and in
1909 Herr Oscar Erbslöh ascended by balloon from St Moritz
Lake to land two days later some 700 miles away, south of
Budapest. The departure was an impressive social occasion,
and the Archduke Ferdinand and his wife turned out to watch
Herr Erbslöh climbing into the gondola. There was a second
ascent in the same year when Captain Messner took off from
St Moritz-Bad to land later in Bohemia. Unhappily, this most
serene and peaceful sport is no longer practised in the Engadine.
Other aeronauts made a fleeting appearance, and the 1911 *Year
Book* reported that:

> Last February Capt. Engelhard appeared with two Wright

aeroplanes and, after repeated failures to fly owing to the
loss of power his engines sustained at this altitude and the
effect the low temperature had on the benzine, he succeeded in remaining in the air for 31 min. 40 sec., piloting
his machine with ease round the lake where he conducted
all his experiments.

The year 1914 started peacefully at St Moritz as elsewhere and,
as one would expect in this superbly hedonist retreat, there was
not the slightest *frisson* of apprehension about the holocaust to
come. The annual *Engadine Year Book* appeared as usual and
the editor confidently solicited advertisements for the 1915
edition. But, though Switzerland remained neutral throughout
the war, the international finance needed for the large tourist
developments which had been accelerating throughout the
Engadine ceased to flow so freely in August 1914, and it was not
only the St Moritz Lake which was frozen. What was St
Moritz like in the last year before the outbreak of the First
World War? How did the visitors pass the Indian summer (and
winter) of the last spacious age?

The previous winter had been a poor one for winter sports.
There were complaints—very unusual for St Moritz with its
high altitude—of a poor snowfall. Wheeled traffic had been
possible at the beginning of March (a bad sign for skiers), but
there had been plenty of sunshine and keen frost. All the hotels,
pensions, and private villas had been crowded throughout the
season, not only in St Moritz but in the other Upper Engadine
villages which were growing in popularity and (though they
would not admit it) benefiting by refraction from St Moritz's
prestige, identified by their golden-sun symbol. Champfer,
Samaden, Pontresina and Celerina were the most obvious
beneficiaries, but growing prosperity was evident in the whole
valley.

An unmistakable sign of the confident economic climate was
provided by the opening of vast new hotels and substantial
additions to existing ones. Suvretta House was opened for

Christmas and was crowded from the start, as was the New Kulm. The Monopol and the Chantarella were also full. In the summer before, Herr Badrutt built an impressive new restaurant at the Palace: in the autumn he opened a new wing, and there were also bachelors' quarters. (This last feature, seldom reproduced, reappeared recently at Courchevel in French Savoy where single male visitors to the Hôtel des Celibataires are waited on by enormous African servants chosen for their gigantic physique and ebony colour.) In December the new Carlton Hotel was opened to rival the Palace, Suvretta House and the Kulm. None has a better situation than the Carlton, looking south-west over the lake, and its formal décor has always been much admired.

Who were the guests who could afford to patronise these palaces of pleasure and who had the energy to make the—now easier—journey to St Moritz? The 1914 records show that in the previous winter and summer seasons a substantial slice of the *Almanach de Gotha*, plus a sprinkling of distinguished commoners, lodged there. In the winter the guests included Prince Max of Baden, Herr Burg-Czuber (ex-Archduke Ferdinand Carl of Austria), three Prince Henrys of Reuss, Prince Maximilian Fürstenberg, the Maharanee Holkar of Indore, Prince Adelbert and Prince Sigismund of Prussia, and the Grand Duke Andreas Vladimirovitch of Russia. As though to prove that blue blood was not vital to stand the altitude, Stanley Baldwin, M.P., stayed at Suvretta House, as did Mrs Lionel Monckton (Gertie Miller), and Hall Caine and Philip Sassoon at the Palace. Percy Lambert, the racing motorist, Sir Henry Seton-Karr, the big-game hunter, and Major Bulpett and J. M. Chambers, who had much to do with starting the Cresta and bob run, were among the more active visitors. Claude Graham White made several flights over the lake with his early bi-plane 'Wake up, England'.

The summer pattern was much the same. The lounge of the Palace Hotel saw Prince Alexis Karageorgevitch (brother of the King of Serbia), and the Czar's cousin, the Grand Duke Peter

Nicolajevitsch of Russia (who came to Glasgow to launch the *Livadia* on the Clyde and called Glasgow 'the centre of the intelligence of England'). The Gaekwar of Baroda and his enormous suite were at Suvretta House, and other very noble nobles to be found at St Moritz were the Prince Broglie, Prince Edward von Liechtenstein, the Princess zu Lowenstein-Westheim, the Marchesa Malvezzi de Medici and the Prince di Savoia. Guests of less princely heritage included Sir Edward Boyle, Sir Alfred Cripps, K.C., Sir Charles Petrie, Mr Leopold de Rothschild, Colonel George Harvey, the President of Harper Brothers (New York), and a fair spread of leading members of the English Bar and Members of Parliament.

No one really knows what they all did. It is strange that, with such a cast and such a setting, St Moritz has attracted little attention from novelists. Should not these Anglo-Saxon favourites Rupert of Hentzau or, more certainly, Rudolf Rassendyll have found their way to glamorous affaires in the Palace or a final duel at the top of Piz Nair? But no English-speaking novelists, not even Dornford Yates and his colleagues who dote on Debrett-like casts, or those who pursue a more picaresque framework, have cast their eyes across the lake to the sun rising over the Corvatsch.

The sad truth is that from the novelist's point of view even in these highly enticing and de-luxe establishments life was by present-day standards incredibly formal. It was agreeable, but it was private. Few of the peccadillos of the peerage committed *in camera* appeared in the Engadine press or, by telegraph, in newspapers in England. There were balls, gala nights, and acceptable Alpine diversions which gradually reached a wider circle, and there were outdoor pursuits, though they were still mostly of a pretty gentle order. But even before the First World War the march of democracy had already penetrated to the visitors' books. An interesting paradox had already begun to manifest itself at St Moritz. As a resort it was *très snob*, but not snobbish. It was, and still is, the microcosm of a mixed but benevolent society. It was not necessary to be descended from the Habsburgs to enjoy the high life there and, while princes and margraves are not seen quite so often nowadays promenading outside Steffani's Hotel, in 1914 and more than fifty years later all visitors behaved as privileged citizens of a unique small kingdom in the Upper Engadine.

The summer season was still the more significant and the *Engadine Year Book* reported objectively that the most important event of the past summer was the opening of a further electrically driven section of the Rhaetian Railway from Bevers to nearby Schuls. After arrival at Schuls

> A procession of guests and prominent inhabitants, headed by a squad of gymnasts, the band, the orchestral society, a number of young ladies dressed in Cantonal colours, and railway officials, marched to the Post-Depot Könz and afterwards to the Hotel Belvedere where a banquet was served to a vast assemblage. The time that passed in doing justice to the repast was pleasantly relieved by the instructive orations that were delivered by the distinguished company of politicians and railway experts.

The next day's programme concluded with a grand procession of groups in character, including the 'Women Defenders of Schuls, as well as miners from the ancient lead and silver mines: hunters, gnomes, fairies and other legendary folk'. Lord Beeching might well have sought the help of the Swiss to stage similar ceremonies to mark the closure of branch lines in Britain.

Mountaineering was the most strenuous summer sport, though never the main feature of St Moritz. Most of the peaks in the Central Bernina Alps had been climbed in the latter half of the last century and there was now a pretty pervasive system of huts, guides' regulations, distress signals, etc. I wonder how many guides were able to invoke paragraph 10 of the Swiss Alpine Club's regulations?

> If two ascents are made in one day, the whole tax will be

charged for the higher peak, and half the tax for the lesser, unless otherwise arranged beforehand.

The pre-1914 season was marked with a fatal accident to a party of four who set off from Diavolezza to ascend Piz Palu. In July the famous guide Christian Zippert made his hundredth accent of Piz Bernina and, as there were several other parties present, the occasion was marked by singing the Swiss National Anthem on the summit.

There had been further improvements, too, for those who came, not to climb mountains, but to enjoy the healing properties of the St Moritz springs. The *Engadine Year Book* proudly proclaimed that:

> The installations for the baths and other apparatus have been carried out according to the most approved modern systems. Last summer the new Kurhaus Baths were opened. Nothing that the highly developed science of hydrotherapy has evolved seems lacking in this beautifully equipped establishment. There are close on 50 bath-rooms. Besides the bath-rooms for use with the waters of St Moritz-Bad there are electric light and vapour baths, inhalation devices, cold and warm douches, etc. All these are administered by well-trained attendants many of whom are also skilled in massage. The baths for the most part are of nickel-plated copper or porcelain.
>
> At the Neues Stahlbad there are 64 bath-rooms, one Scotch douche and one 'Halbbad'. The baths are of bright copper and the water is heated by the Scherrer system which prevents any loss of carbonic acid.
>
> The 'old' and the 'new' springs belong to the Kurhaus while the third, 'Surpunt' belongs to the Neues Stahlbad. The first two have a natural temperature of $5\frac{1}{2}°$, the latter $7°$ Celsius. The water gushes forth in great volume, the 'Surpunt' producing 160 litres a minute.

Lawn tennis was becoming more popular in St Moritz, as

throughout Europe, and this year saw a domino-like increase in
the number of courts and the opening at the Palace Hotel of the
first covered court in Europe. The Swiss championships were
held at the Kulm and *The Alpine Post* strongly deplored the
action of two of the leading players—Robert Kleinschroth,
who retired in the Engadine championship, and Baron von
Bissing, who withdrew from the final of the Swiss championship when 2—1 down in sets. *The Post* rightly contrasted this
supine attitude of giving up when in arrears with the tenacity
of the egregious Mrs Crundall-Punnett who won both the
ladies' championships.

Golf had followed a fitful history at St Moritz since the first
course was laid out in 1891. (John Morris from the St Andrews
family was engaged as professional to the St Moritz Club in
1896: the first professional in Switzerland.) There had been an
amalgamation with the Engadine Golf Club at Samaden where
a splendid enlarged clubhouse had been opened recently, but it
has to be recorded that 'though numerous, the membership of
the Engadine Golf Club was not distinguished by quality'.

It is significant that the account of the winter season lists
skating, tobogganing, curling, bandy, bobsleighing and ski-ing
and ski-joring, in that order of importance. This had been an
exceptionally good season for skating with the St Moritz Lake
frozen over on 23rd November, much earlier than usual. There
had been many developments since Dr Holland, the British
Consul, had concentrated his efforts and teaching in establish-
ing the St Moritz school in 1882. Skating seems to attract the
most contentious of administrators and there were various rival
bodies formed to promote, organise and control skating competitions—always under eminent Englishmen, Sir Coleridge
Grove and the Earl of Lytton being prominent. To the great
majority of skaters, however, it is doubtful whether these
disputes, which were not settled until 1910 when the St Moritz
Skating Association was pleased to combine with the St Moritz
International Skating Club (both almost entirely English
organisations), really meant very much. The every-day skater

would be much more interested in Mr Maxwell Witham's attractive account of skating at St Moritz published in the Badminton volume:

The rinks, which are literally within a stone's throw of the Kulm Hotel, are three in number; the largest, a little over an acre in size, being an irregular square of some eighty yards side. The other two are about half that area. The ice is carefully kept, and whenever the weather will allow, i.e. whenever there is no snow, one or other rink is flooded every night, consequently a visitor generally has a new surface to skate on every morning.

There is no fear of not having sufficient frost. St Moritz is six thousand feet high, and the thermometer usually stands at from 15° to 10° Fahr. from 6 pm to 6 am. Not unseldom it drops below zero in the course of the night. Besides the rink, there is under favourable circumstances most excellent skating to be had on the lakes which run in a chain from the Majola Pass to St Moritz. Under good conditions this is probably the most perfect skating attainable. Exquisite scenery, a clear bright day, and miles of smooth ice so transparent that the stones and fish can be seen yards below. But, like all good things, there is not so much of it as one could wish. A very little wind or a very little snow makes the lakes quite unskateable; and, even without snow, the formation of what are called 'ice flowers' often completely ruins the surface in a few days. Ice flowers arise from the moisture in the air freezing round some point in the ice, and a whole lake will often be found in the morning covered with what at a distance looks like white balls, but which on closer inspection turn out to be clusters and tendrils much like frozen branches of small ferns. They are very beautiful to look at, but very annoying to the skater; moreover, the lake ice after a certain time gets too hard for pleasant skating. Although particularly enjoyable when it comes, the lake skating at St Moritz is something like catching a salmon, chiefly a question of luck. A visitor who spends the whole winter there will probably between one lake and another get a fortnight or so of it. A traveller who runs out from England for a month's holiday will most likely get none at all.

The school of skating at St Moritz is a very severe one: great size, and power and perfect quietness and control of the body and limbs are what is aimed at, and the object throughout is rather to do everything that is attempted in the best possible style than to do a great many different movements moderately.

The unemployed leg is 'kept in its proper place', and the skating at St Moritz is probably the strongest and at the same time the quietest and most accurate that exists. The few accomplished *habitués* of the rink have taken the early teaching of the Skating Club as their starting point, and availing themselves of the long period during which they can practise, have perfected it in a really astonishing manner. Perhaps the weak point of this skating is a certain tendency to stiffness and a slight want of pliability; the skating is, if possible, a trifle too academic, but although the rigid adherence to 'form' in accomplished skaters may detract somewhat from the grace which should always accompany strong and quiet skating, it has the effect of putting young skaters on the right track; and when we see here in England a young skater who may not be able to skate a great many movements, but who does everything he can skate in perfect form, it will be generally found that he has been educated at the St Moritz school.

The winter climate of the Engadine is, taking one year with another, certainly fine, but it is by no means so fine as it is supposed to be. Every year a good amount of snow falls, and a heavy fall, say a foot or eighteen inches, not only stops skating while it is going on, but for two or three days afterwards while it is being cleared away. Only those who have tried it know the labour involved in removing eighteen

inches of snow from an acre of ice. It will probably surprise
many to learn that it will occupy thirty men at least two
days. Moreover, the Engadine is by no means windless,
and the cold which is most enjoyable when the air is still is
almost unendurable when there is a wind, however slight.
On the other hand, there is on the whole much good
weather; and a fine winter's day at St Moritz, with a
bright blue sky and the magnificent mountains sparkling
with snow from summit to base, with its dry thin air which
acts like some ethereal champagne, and a pleasant merry
party skating on perfect ice, is something worth living for.

It was different with the tobogganers on the Cresta, that
most English of all Alpine sports. The first Cresta run was
prepared in the 1884-5 winter by Mr George Robertson, an
Australian, Major W. H. Bulpett and Herr Peter Badrutt, and
the first Grand National race was held in 1885. In the last pre-
war season there was little snow and the run was closed without
any Grand National being run—the first time for twenty-nine
years.

Major Bulpett, by now President of the St Moritz Tobogganing Club, was reported as deprecating the construction of
vertical sidewalls of ice: there had been two fatal accidents
before the run was closed in March. In his view high sidewalls
increased speed so that a rider who did not negotiate a turn
successfully was dashed against the wall out of control, with
possibly serious results. He preferred lower banks, so that if the
rider did not negotiate the bend successfully he would leave the
run (but at a lower speed) and land in snow. His advice was not
heeded.

Curling had been played at St Moritz since 1881 and the St
Moritz Curling Club was formed in 1890. This was a year of
great triumph for the St Moritz Club, who won all the contests
for which they entered, including an exciting win over Grindelwald in the final of the Jackson Cup. On their return from
Grindelwald, the visitors were met with a remarkably elaborate

welcome at the station. A sprightly crowd of sportsmen was gathered on the platform. The Kurverein band in traditional uniform made a clangorous noise and the cup-bearers were driven in a laurel-decked sleigh through cheering crowds to the Kulm, where a great banquet was staged. Ivor Novello could not have conceived anything more sumptuous. The victory was fittingly celebrated in an ode composed by Dr Edgecombe. Something of the ballad's period flavour is evident from the *Year Book*'s quotation:

> Glorious mixture of crimson and yellows
> Paint we the town in a riotous whirl;
> Filling with vast inhalation our bellows,
> Ready in chorus to hurl
> Shouts of ecstatic delight at the jolly good fellows
> Who know how to curl!

Curling is dealt with at length in this book, but the reception given to the Jackson victors is evidence of the particularly English holiday atmosphere which now prevailed beneath the gaze of the Grand Dukes from the windows of the Palace.

Another sport much enjoyed in the winter by natives and visitors alike was bandy: a roughish form of ice hockey. It is not known whether the word 'bandy' comes from the 'bent stick' employed or from the verb 'to bandy', since the ball is 'bandied' about. The game first acquired popularity in the English Fen district where the long stretches of ice are ideal for the game. There are accounts of vigorous games played in the Fens, particularly at Bury Fen, during the great frost of 1812–14, but the first recorded game was held in 1827 between two Fen teams for the stake of a leg of mutton. The game could be played with a ball, maybe a cricket ball, or a primitive puck made of wood or cork. The 'bandies' themselves were natural curved sticks cut from Fen willow trees. The first international match took place in 1891, when a Bury Fen team beat the Netherlands Athletic Union at Haarlem. The rules are rather like those for hockey or association football. The bandy must not be raised above shoulder height and only the goalkeeper could hit the ball in the air. It was a game amateur both in conception and execution and the Badminton volume on skating concluded pontifically that:

> We may expect that in countries blessed with a colder climate the game will develop in the same way as hockey and football have done in England. Play is more rapid and exciting than in any other game. It requires the nicest combined use of eye, hand, and foot, and calls forth the greatest enthusiasm from those who have once played, while to the spectator the rapid and tricky dribbling, accurate passing, and sure shooting, make it a most fascinating spectacle.

Bandy soon flourished in St Moritz. Started by Mr Pennington Legh in the late eighties and 'patronised too by the more energetic and robust of the lady visitors of that year, and especially by Miss Pennington Legh, Miss Vickers and Miss Cook, the game became firmly established in St Moritz two years ago'—thus the *Engadine Year Book* for 1911 pays a well-earned tribute to the hardy Anglo-Saxon ladies who were courageous enough to exchange bandies.

The St Moritz Bandy Club was formed in 1893 with Sir Coleridge Grove as its President. By 1913, however, it was regretfully concluded that the bandy rink should in future be used for ice hockey and played under the auspices of the St Moritz Hockey and Skating Club. It was as though the natives foresaw that some amalgamation would be needed when the visitors were no longer there, as they would not be for the next five years. So much for bandy.

Ski-joring, that strangely masochistic sport where the competitor on skis is pulled by a restless horse across the snow, was also popular at St Moritz. It was started in 1906 by five Norwegians and a race was organised from the Post-Plaz, down the Bahnhofstrasse, through St Moritz-Bad to Champfer, and then back to Steffani's Hotel—much to the peril of any unwary pedestrians. The following year a course was laid out on the frozen lake and ski-joring and trotting races were held. Thereafter there was a rapid increase in the number of horses and bruised ski-jorers. By 1909 the *Year Book* had to warn its readers that:

> Owing to the numerous complaints received by the police of driverless horses being encountered on the public roads it was held desirable to impose a 'test' on members before they were allotted horses for use on the highways. Furthermore, the authorities issued a notice to all livery stable keepers forbidding them to let out horses to people who did not possess the licence issued by the St Moritz Ski-kijöring Club.

4

The Twenties and Thirties

As a climax to the twenties in St Moritz, the second Winter
Olympic Games were held in the village in 1928. The planning
and preparation had taken many years, but the pride of the
Engadine came into her own when the pennants of twenty-five
nations surrounded the Olympic flag, with its five interlocking
rings, flying over the snowbound landscape. St Moritz is better
situated than any other Alpine centre to provide suitable settings
for all the diversions that go to make up the Winter Games,
and it can cope with each event without too wide a dispersal
—a feature much appreciated by spectators. In 1928 the ski-
ing events were confined, as had been those in the Games at
Chamonix four years before, to 'Nordic' events, namely the
long-distance or cross-country run and the ski jump. The
'Alpine' events—the downhill run and the slalom—were later
to be included for the first time at Garmisch-Partenkirchen. As
had been expected, the Scandinavians dominated these events
at the Games, but there was one demonstration which remained
a Swiss speciality and where the Swiss could compete on equal
terms with the Nordic countries. This was the military ski
patrol, which takes place over a distance of 30 km., with an effective climb of at least 1000 metres. Each team consists of four
men (an officer and three other ranks) who have to race wearing
uniform and carrying full military equipment. It is a punishing
contest. This military expertise (which includes shooting) comes
readily to the Swiss Army, whose manœuvres include regular

Cresta Run: Finish Corner

Coming round stream

The great Bibbia on duty

Bibbia off duty

The bob run: building
Horseshoe Bend

A well-built bend

Ventre à terre: A five-man bob travelling head-first
(now no longer practised)

Low round Sunny Corner

Prince Michael of Kent:
A determined bobber

Britain's World Champions:
Tony Nash and Robin Dixon

Gunther Sachs marries Miriam Larsen, 1968:
his fellow-bobbers celebrate

Building the Olympia Schanze

Olympia Schanze: ready
for action

Leaping into space

Soaring like an eagle

practice on skis in this kind of terrain, but teams from other armies are also anxious to compete.

The 1928 race took place on an arduous route from Chantarella, over the Fuorcla Schlattain, down to Corviglia; up over the Fuorcla Saluver, then down to Samaden; along the valley to Punt Muragl Station; then by Lake Staz to finish in St Moritz-Bad. Hard work carrying a heavy pack. The Swiss started slight favourites because they were the defending champions. It was known that the Scandinavian countries had strong, experienced teams, but the Germans were thought to be slightly over-trained. This is a great contest from the spectators' point of view as uniformed soldiers struggle at speed across the exacting course, whether through the streets of Samaden or on the run down to Corviglia. Towards the end of the race, the Norwegians, Finns and Swiss were close together, and partisan cheering became intense, but the Swiss officer lost one of his sticks and, as a result, a lot of time. Norway won, with Finland second, but the place of honour really went to Italy, whose courageous, though inexperienced, team surprised everyone by attacking the course as though inspired by the spirit of the Bersaglieri and finishing fourth.

The other Nordic events comprised the 50 km. race, or marathon, and the 18 km. race, along the north side of the lakes between St Moritz and Maloja. The hazards of the course were greatly increased by a heavy thaw and a severe foehn wind. But justice was done when Per Erik Hedlund, one of the greatest long-distance skiers of all time, won for Sweden, who also finished second and third. Accidents, like a broken ski or binding, can always happen in a strenuous event like this and eliminate worthy competitors, but it requires positive, applied virtue to survive and win. The cross-country ski race is a truly hardy event. The 18 km. race (no one knows why it should be precisely 18 km.) started and finished at the same points as the 50 km., with a sharp climb above Silvaplana and a straight descent to St Moritz-Bad. Norway gained her revenge on the Swedes by occupying the first three places, and runners from

E

the United States and Canada competed in these events for the first time.

The most memorable event at the 1928 Games was the ski jumping on the new Olympia Schanze which had been built two years earlier and now had its official opening. The jump itself, a great, stark gash cut from the trees on the hillside overlooking the lake, was thought at the time to be of frightening proportions. A few figures are needed to illustrate the dimension in which the jumper tests his skill against the elements. From start to take-off the jump is 115 yds. long, with an average incline of 30 degrees: then the jump itself is 120 yds. long, reaching at one point a gradient of 37 degrees. From start to take-off there is a drop of 135 ft. and a total drop of 322 ft. An Austrian has been recorded as reaching a top speed of 85 mph. This is not for the nervous.

The best account of the emotions and tribulations of the jumpers at St Moritz has been given by Sir Arnold Lunn in the *British Ski Book*, 1928:

> Watch a master jumper on the Olympia Schanze, and you will see something which will etch itself into the copperplate of memory. You must stand just above the jump in order to appreciate the full horror of the view which confronts the jumper just as he approaches the platform, the sense of an unplumbed void below and the far infinite distance of the valley.
>
> A bell rings. Number 1 jumps round swiftly and darts down to the platform. He passes us crouching. Your heart bleeds for him. Swiftly, rhythmically, he uncoils. He has left the solid ground which the Creator intended for his playground, and you see him for one brief moment released like an arrow from a bow. And so he disappears from view.
>
> And now walk down the hill and take up your station just below the platform. A sudden rush of wind and here comes No. 2. The flaps of his tightly drawn coat beat in the

wind as the air pressure forces itself into every cranny of his garments. In these long jumps, the sound made by the jumper in the air is, at least, as terrifying as the sight of a man alighting from the air, a sound like an angry eagle flapping its wings before pouncing on its prey.

Watch him as he dives through the empty chambers of the sky, his body bent forward, his hands grasping as it were for the ski points. Infinite time seems to pass. Will he never land?

Smack! Nine feet of hickory have made contact with the snow, hard-beaten and polished like marble.

Will he stand? Quick as thought comes the answer. A momentary swerve, every muscle in his magnificent body fighting for control. The struggle is short, sharp and decisive. One erring ski, seeking divorce from its fellow, is wrenched back into line. The backward tug is overcome. Erect, controlled and rejoicing, the jumper sails down the run-out, forces his ski breadthwise into the snow and swings to rest, while the Referee signals '70 metres gestanden,' and a thousand voices roar their applause.

The educational effect of sport does not begin and end with the competitors. One cannot dismiss the 'Publikum' as a collection of corpulent, over-fed patrons of luxurious hotels. The thrills which we witnessed at St Moritz have a far-reaching effect upon the mind. One returns from seeing Thams jump with a new pride in the race to which one belongs, the human race. The essence of all sport is the duel between the spirit of men and the limitations of matter. A record jump stirs one like noble music. There is the same intangible sense of the finite at war with the infinite, of the unattainable towards which mankind strives, that undiscovered country whose frontier alone is dimly sighted from the Pisgah heights of high endeavour.

It is good to know that one more conquest has been registered in the struggle between man and his environment, that the mastery over mind and muscle has once again been found a beautiful and satisfying mode of expression.

Man is never satisfied, and the jumper will always strive to beat his own best performance. The struggle for the record jump will inevitably proceed, and the jumper will continue to hurl himself further and further into space undeterred by those who desire to fix a limit, 'thus far and no farther'.

On the occasion described by Sir Arnold, the Norwegian Tullin Thams made a demonstrably superhuman effort to reach what was, by the standards of the day, the incredible distance of 73 metres. Unfortunately, he landed as he had taken off, slightly to the right, which marred the utter perfection of his jump, and he fell in that direction. Sir Arnold shrewdly observed this occasion as symbolising the aspirations not only of ski jumpers but of all earth-bound mortals. The apparently motionless figure, hands firmly to his sides, leaning at once forward and upward into the air, soared like Icarus into the heavens, leaving terrestrial worries behind. Nothing demonstrated more clearly both man's courageous attempt to challenge the very atmosphere and the limitations he faced. But Thams' jump also had a more precisely contemporary significance. During the few seconds when the laws of gravity were apparently defied and the spectators could identify themselves with him, it was as though they were shaking themselves free from the preoccupations of the twenties and the depression spreading throughout Europe.

For depression there was. It was now pretty apparent that the attempt, after the end of the First World War, to create a land fit for heroes to live in had failed, not only in Britain, but throughout the Continent. The rundown of the economy and the eventual flight from the gold standard need no exposition, nor does it require any great hindsight to detect at least the psychological reasons for the maladies of the twenties. The great, or at least the effective, majority was not prepared to contemplate the wholesale changes in the fabric of society which were needed. There was, indeed, a tendency to look nostalgically at what seemed a happier pre-war existence, and to think of restoration as preferable to reinvigoration. There was, too, a willingness to believe the aphorisms and panaceas of political leaders, because few were prepared to face up to the unpalatable alternatives. Some glimpses of the social scene and the entertainment world in England are not out of place, because it is entertainment at St Moritz in all its aspects, and its appeal to the English, that we are really looking at.

First the circuses, or, rather, the one great circus of the twenties—the British Empire Exhibition opened at Wembley in 1924 with all the pomp and circumstance that could be mustered. Perhaps the last overripe flowering of the imperial myth, it was notable for the most bizarre collection of architectural monstrosities ever assembled and, as a focal point, the unprecedented sight of a life-size statue of the Prince of Wales, made of butter. The quaint buildings within the Wembley curtilage offered an escape from the humdrum and growing disappointment of the twenties. But others found their refuge and relaxation in the Swiss snow—just as the early English mountaineers had made for the Alps as an antidote to the overwhelming materialism of the Victorians.

As an age, the twenties were much concerned with speed and sport. These were the years of Captain Malcolm Campbell, racing on the Pendine Sands, and his rival, Sir Henry Segrave, breaking records in his Golden Arrow. Alan Cobham was flying to the Cape of Good Hope and back in record time and before the end of the twenties Lindbergh made his solo flight across the Atlantic. Paradoxically, it was also an era of elegance at Wimbledon, dominated by the genius of Suzanne Lenglen, and a high summer for English cricket. In the same season you could see Jack Hobbs, the diffident craftsman, breaking W. G. Grace's record of 125 centuries in first-class cricket; Herbert Sutcliffe reminding us anew of the determined concentration

that only Yorkshiremen can display; Patsy Hendren, the true
professional; Frank Woolley, the graceful and authoritative; and
the most genial of all-rounders, Maurice Tate. The English
press seemed determined to concentrate on easeful days at
Lord's to the exclusion of growing economic depression.

Despite the mannered deportment of the cricket field, still
cherished and revered by the British public, it was an age of
hysteria where novelty and sensation were eagerly sought. True,
the entertainment provided on the new medium, the wireless,
was harmless enough, and no one derived anything but gentle
amusement from the most popular comedians (now, alas, on
their way to oblivion), Leonard Henry, Stainless Stephen,
Clapham and Dwyer, and Tommy Handley; or from Reginald
Foort, the cinema organist; or Albert Sandler and the Palm
Court Orchestra; or the leading dance band of the day, the
Savoy Orpheans, who in 1924 made history by broadcasting
from an aeroplane flying over Croydon.

Underneath, however, there was something more frenzied.
The second half of the twenties was the twilight of the Bright
Young Things, who carried out their crepuscular activities until
dawn. Chaperons had almost completely disappeared, and this
was the age of the bottle party, the floor show—The Midnight
Follies at the Hotel Metropole, with a cast which included
Beatrice Lillie and June, was probably the first—the nightclub
and the Charleston. When it first appeared in 1925 the Charleston was thought to be too *outré* even for the twenties, but it
became popular as soon as it was danced by the Prince of Wales.
It is worth recalling how, ever since his world tour in 1919, he
had been the glass of fashion and the mould of form.

Among the nightclubs which sprouted throughout Mayfair,
those promoted by Kate Meyrick (Brett's, the '43', and so on)
led the fashion. So much was she in the public eye that, as Mr
John Montgomery observed in his penetrating analysis of *The
Twenties*, when released from a short gaol sentence her followers
were invited to:

Come all you birds
And sing a roundelay,
Now Mrs Meyrick's
Out of Holloway.

It is doubtful if theirs was a typical reaction. There were many more to echo the mood of John Betjeman's faded nightclub queen.

There was sun enough for lazing upon beaches,
There was fun enough for far into the night;
But I'm dying now and done for,
What on earth was all the fun for?
I'm old and tired and terrified and tight.

The cinema and the theatre were likewise dominated by escapism. The early twenties were ruled by Valentino with *The Four Horsemen*, *The Sheik*, *Blood and Sand* and *Monsieur Beaucaire*. Then came such splendid, though scarcely serious, entertainers as Harold Lloyd, Tom Mix and Douglas Fairbanks, until Al Jolson's *The Jazz Singer* killed the silent film with a single blow. By now, the melancholy, off-key voice of Noël Coward was heard on the stage: *The Vortex* in 1925; *This Year of Grace* in 1928; and the soft-centred confection called *Bitter Sweet* in 1929. The theatre had an unending appetite for the lightest form of entertainment. Jack Buchanan and June in *Boodle* at the Empire; *No, No, Nanette* at the Palace; Charlot's Revue at the Prince of Wales; and Tom Walls and Ralph Lynn starting their long resident career at the Aldwych. Although there was no computerised Top of the Pops, the most popular tunes of the times ranged from such musical masterpieces as 'Yes, we have no bananas' to the delicate lyric of 'Horsy, keep your tail up' and the virile scoring of 'The Riff Song'.

The main contemporary writers reflected the mood of the time. Only George Bernard Shaw could vie in influence with Aldous Huxley, and there was not much hope for the future in the cavortings of Theodore Gumbril and Mrs Viveash in *Antic*

Hay (1923) or in *Brave New World* (1932). D. H. Lawrence, Somerset Maugham, Michael Arlen; none could be described as preaching an over-optimistic message: nor could the poets, under the already overriding influence of T. S. Eliot. There were also what might be described as routine female novelists of the type set by Ethel M. Dell and Ruby M. Ayres; not to mention the historical novels of Hugh Walpole which, even in their day, were regarded as too traditional to be alive.

It was from such a background that the English traveller in the late twenties would board the boat-train at Victoria on the first stage of his journey to St Moritz. During the 1920s St Moritz was not immune from the financial crises which affected various parts of Europe, but by the second half of the decade it was gearing itself to prepare for its first Winter Olympic Games. The visitor would have found an air of activity. The hoteliers, the Kurverein, and all concerned with St Moritz's welfare were busy refurbishing as far as was needed to be ready to act as hosts to the large numbers expected at the beginning of 1928.

The visitor who oriented himself from the centre of the Post-Platz would see, first, Steffani's Hotel. Steffani's is one of the oldest hotels in St Moritz and still preserves many of the features shown in the earlier Victorian daguerrotypes. It was the favourite haunt of the curlers from the St Moritz Club who, even if they did not always stay there, were certainly to be seen often enough inside, refreshing themselves after the day's ardours. The ski guides, too, were most often found there ready to exchange advice and carefully chosen extracts from local mythology. Steffani's was always a highly individual establishment, from the bedrooms on the top floor overlooking the St Moritz Lake, to the recondite activities in the Grotto in the basement. Moving west along the top road, the next hostelry is the Hotel Bernasconi, owned and directed by the family of that name. The Bernasconi is a smaller hotel but has preserved its own reputation for a high-class regional cuisine. This was the place for fondue parties and in later years it was much patronised by the musical world; both Herbert von Karajan and Vittorio de Sabata were welcome guests. Next, the Bella Vista, perched on the southern side and looking towards the sun, before you reach the Segantini Museum (of which more later) and start the agreeable mile walk to Suvretta House.

Suvretta House has always contrived to be both inside and outside St Moritz. It takes about half an hour to reach it on foot from St Moritz and about twenty minutes going downhill on the return journey. Suvretta is almost a tourist resort in itself. Built by the Bon family in 1912, it affects an architectural style which is eclectic but otherwise defies any accurate description. It cannot be called, simply, Engadiner, and there is no distinctive Grisons style which suits it. Perhaps a location on the banks of the Rhine might really have been more appropriate. But, once inside, the comfort of the guests is well provided for. An entrance hall, and lounge which looks as though it had been removed from a Habsburg palace; a remarkable, urbane restaurant where the only problem is the heat of the sun at lunchtime; and a Grill Room (for those who require something still more *exclusive*) which would not be out of place in the George V in Paris. The Suvretta does its guests proud and looks after all their outdoor activities as well—curling, ski-ing or skating.

Starting from the Post-Platz, the visitor who did not wish to contemplate an immediate visit to Suvretta might go eastwards towards the territory sacred to the bob and Cresta riders. High on the hill to his left he would see the Hotel Chantarella on its own escarpment. The Chantarella, also built before the First World War, sits on a sparkling little plateau overlooking its private ice-rink. With its sunny situation, it was originally designed as a sanatorium, but such was its popularity (and, no doubt, the successful treatment provided there) that it soon became an hotel in its own right. But many would find the climb to Chantarella too steep to walk and would either hire a horse-drawn sleigh and make a gentle way up the winding slopes or use the Corviglia cable car and alight at the first stop.

On the way to the bob run comes, first, the Hotel Albana,
built into the front of the main shopping area. The Rosatsch and
Monopol, always a favourite with the English, come next, and
then there is the Hotel Eden, formerly the Petersburg whose
advertised attractions included an 'English billiards table'. By
now the visitor has almost passed the temptations of the
jewellers' shops and enticing boutiques and has reached the
plateau whereon stands the Engadiner Kulm, the largest hotel
in St Moritz. The Kulm was the original base of the Badrutt
family and the oldest part dates from 1856, with extensions
added in 1870 and 1909. The Kulm rightly claims to offer great
comfort, but it affects no great homogeneity in architectural
styles. From the outside there is a quaint mixture of Swiss,
Venetian or Turkish and art nouveau. Behind this variegated
façade the Kulm is furnished with a unique collection of old
Swiss furniture and pictures. In its shapely central hall bobbers
and Cresta riders congregate every evening to see the results of
the day's runs and the orders for the following day posted. A
Grill Room which, in the author's view, provides unrivalled
Swiss food, and the Sunny Bar, one of the original homes of the
'bar dancing', are among its other features.

The visitor's third route takes him across the Post-Platz to the
Schweizerhof, which preserves a Victorian façade dating from
the time of its construction at the end of last century. There
used to be a time when the noise of the pipes in the Schweizerhof's heating system was one of the principal sounds in St
Moritz, but this has now, happily, been cured. The Schweizerhof looks straight over the St Moritz Lake and its main frontage
is decorated throughout the winter with an enormous statue
carved out of snow (often a rabbit). Farther down the road,
towards the railway station, comes the Palace, which proudly
asserts that it is the most luxurious hotel in Switzerland. It
probably is. Certainly there is no elegant, expensive or esoteric
activity that is not catered for. The high ceiling of the main
lounge emphasises the effect of a temple sacred to Mammon,
and this effect is not entirely dispelled in the restaurant, the

bars, or even the bowling alley. Few can aspire to visit the Palace, but no one will forget his stay there. Just below the Palace there is a slightly cosier establishment called the Hotel La Margna. Inside its strange honeycomb frontage it offers a genuine Engadiner atmosphere, and evening entertainment is liberally garnished with folklore, musical and otherwise. It provides an interesting contrast to the baroque splendour of the Palace. From this road the visitor would see the Carlton, opened just before the First World War and the last of the really plush establishments built at that time. It has possibly the best situation in the whole of St Moritz-Dorf. On a promontory overlooking the lake, it does not miss a single ray of sunshine. The atmosphere is strangely formal and the clientele is more European than English.

5

Curling

Curling at St Moritz is one of the really enjoyable amateur pastimes. Praise of this kind is a matter of degree. It is very marginal what makes the ambience of Harry's Bar in Venice, or the Polo Bar at London's Westbury, or (now, unhappily, no more) the Bar Leland at Florence, so much more enticing than elsewhere. Not even the most accomplished sybarite, nor the most consistent addict, has explained the difference convincingly, but it exists. In much the same way, St Moritz is the place for the true amateur. The curling is not so ruthlessly organised as at Zermatt. The stones are not laid out with dreadful, mathematical symmetry every morning before the sun comes up—the St Moritz iceman is more likely to be obstinately brushing overnight snow off the rink as the first curlers climb up from the village. The casual, diffident atmosphere is part of the attraction, and occasional professional skill is carefully masked. But it would be wrong to give the impression that curling is not a serious sport demanding the keenest application while an 'end' is in progress.

Curling came late to Switzerland. There is some dispute whether the game first started in Holland or in Scotland. There was a game in Holland called *kluyten*, or *kalluyten*, played on ice, as was the Icelandic *knattleikr*, but the resemblance to curling is not very well established. Two paintings by Pieter Brueghel (1530–1569) do, however, appear to show an activity like curling taking place. It is perhaps surprising that when the Scottish Parliament, in 1457, were applying their minds to the prohibition of unnecessary, and unprofitable, sports and ordained that golf and football should be 'cryit dune' they did not mention curling. But it is clear that one of the earliest curling stones, much cruder than the polished precision ones now in use, is the Stirling stone, still preserved, and dated 1511. Thereafter there are frequent references to curling and curlers in Scottish history, including George Grahame, the Bishop of Orkney, who in 1638 was charged with the grievous crime of being 'a curler on the ice on the Sabbath day'.

There is no doubt that curling is emphatically a Scottish game either by origin, which seems likely, or, if not, by early adoption. In the year of the first Jacobite Rebellion (1715) Dr Pennecuick opined that:

> To Curle on the Ice does greatly please,
> Being a Manly Scottish Exercise;
> It clears the Brains, stirrs up the Native Heat
> And gives a gallant Appetite for Meat.

A century and a half later the Royal Caledonian Curling Club could make the bland claim that:

> The introduction of curling into countries furth of Scotland has always been the work of Scotsmen. While other nationalities have readily taken up the game, its progress has chiefly depended on Scotsmen.

This arrogant assertion seems fully justified, and Scots still act as instructors and often organise curling at Swiss resorts.

Scotland has supplied stones for curling throughout the world, since no other country seems to have stone of the right geological structure. Professor Foster-Heddle, an eminent Victorian geologist, is quoted in the Badminton chapter on curling with some profound observations on the stone most suitable for curling:

> The excellence of any one rock depends upon the relative amount of the hard, heavy, and tough ingredients; upon their relative firm adhesion one to the other, through a

promiscuous interlocking of the component crystals, and to uniformity in structure throughout. *Ceteris paribus*, the smaller the grain the better.

He goes on to itemise the best stones, in order of merit, with the sonorous names of Burnock Water, Crawfordjohn, Ailsa Hone, Crieff Black, Carsphairn, Crieff Serpentine and Tinkernhill, and of these he preferred the Ailsa Hone. Nowadays, the island of Ailsa Craig off the Ayrshire coast is still a primary source for the supply of stone. The finished article weighs between 35 lb. and 40 lb., and the curler must ensure that it never loses its gloss and brilliant polish. If polished and properly cut, the heaviest stone can be controlled on the ice; otherwise the effort of delivering it is heavy and frustrating. It is the practice to cut a hollow out of the two flat sides of the stone so that it actually runs on a rim. Stones are reversible, and one side has a smaller rim for keen ice, while the reverse side carries a larger one for use when the ice is dull or slow.

In Scotland, curling still achieves the status of a truly national sport once a year when, provided there is sufficient frost, a Grand Match is organised between the North and South. Six hundred rinks of four-a-side take part on one of three lochs in central Scotland where there is a possibility of sufficient depth of ice being available. The Grand Match is organised by the Royal Caledonian Curling Club, the game's parent body, and one whose global authority is less frequently challenged than is that of the Royal and Ancient Club at St Andrews in the golfing world. The Rev. John Kerr, in his *History of Curling* (1890), records that when Queen Victoria was being entertained by the Earl of Mansfield, then President of the club, she asked how the game was played. The noble Earl showed how to throw stones on the floor of the ballroom of Scone Palace, and the Monarch, *mirabile dictu*, attempted to throw a stone. A pleasantly droll picture, which may not have been appreciated by those who had to re-polish the floor. For curlers, the attraction of the game is perennial. Witness the words of John Cairnie (he called his country house 'Curling Hall'), the royal club's first President in 1838, who replied to a toast in his honour by saying:

> I am now an old curler, and very unable to speak as I should like; but I am a keen curler; the spirit is willing but the flesh is weak. I think I shall curl to the last.

The eighteen playing rules prescribed by the royal club are commendably short, occupying only a few pages, and have changed little over the last century. They are concerned with such basic essentials as marking out the rink (46 yds. long), drawing the circles at each end, and the delivery of the stones. Thereafter it is up to the skip and his three colleagues to throw their stones, sweep them to the required spot (or marker, or dolly)* and lay subsequent stones as guards to obstruct the enemy, or strike out opposing stones. The ice will resound to the skip's direction of 'inhandle', or 'outhandle', according to which turn is to be imparted to the stone to affect the course of its progress. Then there will be emphatic shouts of 'soop', or 'bruschen', as the sweepers are exhorted to polish the ice with their brushes in the path of the oncoming stone to make it go farther and to straighten its course.

There has been little alteration in the system of play at St Moritz from the 1880s onwards. The first player in the team of four, preferably with a pair of heavy stones, will play them so that they draw up on the forward edge of the 'house' of concentric rings outside which no stone counts. The second player will protect them by laying a guard—provided that the enemy has not meanwhile got nearer the centre of the house. By the time the third player's turn comes, some of the opposition's stones will be lying in such a way that he must 'wick', or deflect from them, or dislodge them. Lastly, the skip himself has either to remove the opponent's preferred shot or lay one himself. All

* The dolly, which marks the tee (centre of the circles), is used only in Continental Europe and Scandinavia. It comes in various shapes and sizes and is often brightly coloured.

depends on the skip's directions, and he has the last word; that is, his own shot. The skip must be a man of authority, imperturbable when his plot comes unstuck, and capable of showing a real quality of leadership. His moment of triumph comes when he plays the last stone, and follows it up the ice as it is brushed into the house under the direction of the No. 3, who takes temporary charge. It lies 'shot', and all the players raise their brooms in the air to acclaim him.

An eight-end at curling is even rarer than is a hole-in-one at golf. One such occurrence is recalled in the St Moritz Club's records when the skips were the Hon. F. N. Curzon and F. H. (later Lord Chancellor) Maugham. The last end of the afternoon was played with snow falling and, as the rink became slower, the players could get their stones up to the house but no farther than the dolly. This produced the remarkable sight of sixteen stones in one half of the house—a proposition which the Lord Chancellor, if it had been brought before him, might have thought to lack credibility.

The game has its own vocabulary, and that early authority, the Rev. John Kerr, illustrated this to explain:

> A ridge along the ice is a *sow's back*, a lazy stone which grunts and settles down too soon is a *hog*, a stone which once down remains in spite of all attempts to move it is a *clockin-hen*.

The Rev. Mr Kerr also referred, with approval, to a wife who had been known more than once, to carry, or wheel, her husband's curling stones to a pond miles distant when he was unable to do so himself, although able to play when he reached the ice.

The poet Allan Ramsay has a felicitous phrase about a Scottish nobleman who would 'run rejoicing with his curling throw'. Called the 'roarin' game' because of the distinctive noise which the stone makes on its way across the ice, there is plenty of roaring by the participants. It is no wonder that in such an atmosphere James Hogg, the Ettrick shepherd, could describe how:

> Here peer and peasant friendly meet,
> Auld etiquette has lost her seat,
> The social broom has swept her neat
> Beyond the pale o' curling.

Nowhere is this truer than beneath the blue skies of the Engadine. Most developments in curling in the last hundred and fifty years have been in the growth of artificial rinks and, more recently, indoor ice-rinks. There it is possible to guarantee a more uniform consistency of ice; the stones are sharpened for accuracy, and a sliding delivery is affected by the experts. Such developments tend to be treated with affectionate scorn by the true amateur who relishes the exhilaration of curling in the open air where the sun and the wind can change the texture and level of the ice between ends—just to make it more difficult.

In 1890 the Rev. Mr Kerr had written:

> At one place in Switzerland, 6,000 feet above sea-level, curling, we believe, has been introduced. But we hear of no club having been formed in that country: and where no club is formed, curling never seems to succeed.

For once, the reverend sportsman's intelligence was at fault. The St Moritz Curling Club, the premier club in Switzerland, was in fact founded in 1880, although there had been curling at St Moritz for some years before. By the 1899–1900 season, sixty players took part in the club competition, and they were all visitors except for one of the Badrutt family. Grindewald followed before the turn of the century, and soon after there were flourishing clubs at Arosa, Celerina, Mürren, Villars and Wengen. The St Moritz Club records show that in the 1902–3 season members started curling on 18th November on the Statzer See, a small pond two miles away which is regularly the first to freeze. On 10th December a full rink was in operation on the frozen St Moritz Lake; by the 14th December curling had started on the club's own rink; and the final game in that season did not take place until 19th March, four months after the start. As a measure of the game's popularity, 1908 saw a five-day

F

Bonspiel at Celerina, the fourth to be held in Switzerland. Twelve rinks competed, and the Archduke Franz Ferdinand of Austria threw the first stone. The St Moritz rink, skipped by a Scot, Mr James Craig, were the winners. By 1911 it was also reported that a lot of strong players were tucked away at Samaden and Celerina.

The St Moritz Club retains its primacy, and its own particular flavour. It leases a rink from Herr Badrutt near the Kulm, in what is called Badrutt's Park, adjacent to the skating rink, where the graceful spectacle of the lady skaters sometimes distracts curlers from their proper business, and the wooden clubhouse and verandah provide a very discernible link with earlier Victorian curlers. It is said that curling, like much else at St Moritz, started with some characteristically energetic activity on the part of Caspar Badrutt, then manager of the Kulm Hotel. A Scotsman gave him a present of a pair of stones and a copy of the Royal Caledonian Club's annual. Badrutt soon set to work: the stones were copied by local craftsmen and a rink was laid out. By 1890, the St Moritz Club had been formed with an entirely Anglo-Saxon committee—H. C. Kennard, H. W. Topham, T. A. Cook, F. de B. Strickland and H. B. Kent.

The club's rules are not oppressive and are really designed to ensure that visitors are welcome, particularly if they come with someone wearing the small enamel badge in the shape of a curling stone which indicates membership: or, even more, if they are accompanied by a committee member wearing the tie of black, grey and gold, which was certainly not selected for aesthetic reasons. There will be much crowding round the single stove in the saloon of the clubhouse (it has to be admitted that it is now a pretty rackety building) until someone drives everyone on to the ice to stand to his broom and be allocated to a rink. That someone for many years has been Billy Griggs.*

Billy is the true familiar spirit of St Moritz and epitomises all that is amusing and generous. He owns to being over eighty, but most curlers think that he has been supervising the rinks

* Unfortunately Billy Griggs has since died.

since the Almighty decreed that curling should start. A jockey in his youth, he welcomes novices; gives them a few quick lessons—'Bring the stone back on the same line as you send it forward, and don't drop it to crack the ice'—and is only happy when he has found everyone a place. Then, and only then, he has been known to dance gently in an elf-like way on the ice to the piped music relayed for the benefit of the skaters next door Less agile than he used to be, there is no more engaging sight than Billy's weatherbeaten face smiling under his fur hat pulled down over his ears.

Later in the day he refreshes himself at Steffani's Bar, and can be moved to tell valiant tales which date from the beginning of time. One of his favourite anecdotes recalls his service with the Duke of Westminster's squadron in Egypt during the First World War. His Grace told Billy that he was going on leave to Cairo to have some uniforms fitted, and that he should come too. So Billy made his way down Soliman Pasha with the great Bend'Or, who ordered two suits for him at the same time; but Billy had something else in mind. The Egyptian Derby was soon due at the Gezira Club: Billy made some enquiries, secured a mount and, after some preliminary schooling, decided that he was on a good thing. He wagered all his pay on a win. Predictably, he outrode the local jockeys, and returned to his regiment with two new Service dress suits and £130: 'And then,' he would remember ruefully, 'Griggs was better off than ever before, or since.' Worthy Billy, St Moritz salutes you.

Under Billy's direction the rinks are busy till lunchtime, with the sun changing the texture of the ice as it rises over the Corvatsch. The remarkable effect which the sun can have is one of the most fascinating aspects of outdoor curling. A few rays from the sun seem sufficient to transform ice, which has been so fast that stones can scarcely be controlled on it, to a sluggish surface on which they will sit down like pancakes. It can also produce ridges, or affect the level of the ice so that the stone will not curl in one particular direction. No one can curl to perfection, but a newcomer—and few have more than ten days or a fortnight's curling—can soon acquire sufficient skill to enjoy himself. More than many games, curling combines scientific, or at least mathematical, principles with fairly complete simplicity of application. Maybe a dozen ends are played; more active than appears, for the vigorous polishing of ice under the skip's direction requires the use of muscles never otherwise used, and many a curler on his first night has been convinced that he has cracked a rib or maybe torn a ligament. Then, to either the Scala or the Kulm Sunny Bar for a glass of grog, or gluhwein, before lunch.

If the sun is bright, lunch will be on the club's verandah; a picnic, fetched by the curler from his hotel—a few slices of wunderfleisch perhaps, some Emmenthal cheese, finished with some coffee and a glass of kirsch from the bar of Badrutt's skating rink. There follows half an hour's relaxation and contemplation of the ice: one of the moments of well-being. Well exercised, well refreshed, the relaxed curler will think of himself as at one with great curlers of the past. More than that, as he watches the patterns of light on the peaks on either side of the valley he will identify himself with the unchanging landscape and in some indefinable way feel a temporary sense of being lifted out of himself. The poet Wordsworth was not a curler, but he must have had something of this in mind when he described the sensation of being 'rolled round in earth's diurnal course with rocks, and stones, and trees'. But the afternoon kip is soon over. Billy will call his curlers back to earth, or ice, and a few more ends (possibly more desultory than in the morning) until it is time to put away the stones, lock the brooms in the clubhouse, and off to Hanselmann's or Hauser's for tea.

Only occasionally will the retreating curler engage in subversive activities like the one who, passing one of the elegant shoe shops on the hill down to Hanselmann's, was surprised to see a crowd waiting outside. He enquired the reason:

'We are waiting to see the Shah of Persia and the Empress when they come out.'

'In that event,' he replied, 'you must demonstrate. Never wait in a crowd without organising a protest.'

'But what should we protest about?'

'The price of caviar.'

The younger members of the crowd took this to heart, and the Shah (as reported in the European press) was perplexed to be greeted by loud cries of 'Cheaper caviar; cheaper caviar'. A serious political demonstration, entirely appropriate to the refined atmosphere of the Engadine.

The photographs of past Chairmen, which hang on the walls of the clubhouse of the Curling Club, tell their own story. They are mostly British, although there is no discrimination on nationalist grounds and the Swiss, Germans and Austrians are represented. But for the most part they come from the British Services, the professions or the City, or—as befits the origin of the game—from Scottish farms. Colonel Krabbe, Sir Louis Gluckstein, Sir John Corry and Ian Campbell of Balblair in the remote north-west of Scotland are good examples. Campbell, a great sheep farmer in his day, was one of the most minatory skips and, in distinctive Doric, commanded his rink as though they were recalcitrant ewes. When someone invited him to throw a glove down on the ice, as is often done to mark the target for the next stone, he retorted with growing choler: 'Glove! That's something I've never owned.' Few could really be so impervious to the cold air.

Ian Campbell was also much involved in one of the club's favourite myths. Many years ago a party of jockeys arrived in St Moritz from England and were unable to get a game on the ice. This was partly because the rinks were full (it was the height of the season) and partly because they were then comparatively unknown, and there were, to put it innocently, a number of misunderstandings. But the jockeys were not to be denied. They adopted the same course as other sportsmen have done when they wanted to join in some particular game. They paid frequent visits to the bar at Steffani's Hotel, the most popular headquarters of the curlers; they were hospitable and generous; they kept the conversation turning towards the possibility of curling at the St Moritz Club; and they offered a persistent challenge to any four to play a match with them for a very sizable stake. Eventually, their persistence was rewarded and the challenge could no longer be avoided. The jockeys withdrew to their hotel, well satisfied that they had gained their first objective. On the following day, against all the odds (Ladbrokes would not have given much for their chances), the jockeys won, and returned to Steffani's to place the stake money on the bar for the free entertainment of all who were present. Time passed; two of the jockeys (not now to be named) were well refreshed; Ian Campbell, alarmed for their safety, took them up, one under each arm—as he was accustomed to lift Black-face sheep in his native Sutherland—and carried them across the square to their hirsel at the Schweizerhof.

Since then, Sir Gordon Richards has been a popular and acceptable Chairman of the St Moritz Club, and has shown himself as accomplished in the 'house' as he was at the finishing post. Douglas Smith is an equally skilful curler, and the turf has also been well represented by Scobie Breasley and the Hide brothers. From another sporting field, Joe Davis made a spectacular appearance on the ice some years ago. Though he had few pretensions to the finer points of curling, he had such a good eye as a snooker player that he could direct his stone through 'ports', or gaps, that no one else would attempt. But, for my money, D. Smith was the man.

But the St Moritz Club does not provide the only facilities for the Roarin' Game in the village. The inquisitive visitor, standing on the icy eminence that marks the start of the bob run, can not only look due west to see the St Moritz clubhouse, almost under the shadow of the semi-Venetian façade of the Kulm Hotel and adjacent to the antics of the skaters on Badrutt's Kulm ice-rink, he can also look due south towards the massive frontage of the Carlton Hotel and there, lower down, are the spacious rinks of the Engiadina Club founded in 1920.

The Engiadina has always attracted more Swiss, and other European, than English visitors, possibly because they are curlers who practise their favourite sport throughout the winter instead of, like the Anglo-Saxons, during a brief holiday. Here the curling is sharper. There is more professional skill, and the accuracy of the Engiadiners is their deliberate answer to the diffident amateurism of the St Moritz Club members. Here, too, the formalities of the curling rules are strictly, though amicably, observed. There are important competitions with teams from elsewhere, and the composition of the rinks is carefully balanced; but there is no less sport. For those who want serious curling in the most encouraging and experienced company and in dramatic surroundings, under the shadow of the bob run, this must surely be their objective. The Engiadina Club is exceptionally well organised and has ambitious plans for an artificially covered rink for the future. It serves to remind visitors that the Swiss have been curling for the whole of this century, and are prepared to take on all comers.

There are two hotel rinks, at Chantarella and Suvretta House, which provide their own variety. The Chantarella rink is a small one, with the most favoured situation of all. In front of the Chantarella Hotel, it has been built on the edge of the escarpment which looks down on the village. Curlers can gaze from their lofty plane east to Celerina and Samaden, or west right up the valley towards the Maloja. The Chantarella rink is, perhaps, the very fulcrum of St Moritz. Everything falls away from it on one side or another. The curling, mainly by hotel guests, is relaxed and informal.

The Suvretta House rink is much more ambitious. At the bottom of the Suvretta ski-run, skiers coming down the slopes sometimes look as though they would end up on the ice and scatter the stones. The rink is on the very edge of the Suvretta territory; deer have been seen near it at night. By day there is a panoramic, but distant, view towards Champfer. The ice, to the author's mind, is uncannily good. How can ice vary perceptibly? It may be the way the foundations are laid and frozen; it may be the patience of the iceman who sprays and re-sprays the surface. Whatever the reason, there have been many visitors to Suvretta who say that they have never found better ice.

Suvretta House manage to run their ice-rink like everything else, with an Olympian lack of concern for the rest of St Moritz. They have their own domestic competitions during the season, but they also welcome contests with visitors from elsewhere. Veterans from the St Moritz Club manage to transport their stones to Suvretta for an occasional battle, and they find curlers of like mind waiting for them—guests from all over Europe who survive in the stylish atmosphere of Suvretta House.

Lord Fraser (Hugh Fraser of Harrods fame) was for long one of Suvretta's favourite guests. (It was while staying at St Moritz that Lord Fraser first thought of his highly individual plan for developing the winter sports centre at Aviemore in the Scottish Highlands.) Towards lunchtime, the rink would re-echo with Fraser's unmistakable Scottish cry of 'Here comes the humdinger', as he launched a fierce stone to finish the final end. The Shah, whose villa is very near the rink, has been known to peer over the edge, obviously bewildered at such a strange manifestation of enthusiasm.

In this chapter we started with early curling in Scotland and end with a distinguished Scotsman curling at St Moritz. A merry partnership between the two countries, much to the advantage of both. Curlers, old and young, men and women—this is not a sport which practises sexual segregation and, as at croquet, ladies are often more vicious and determined at knocking the enemy out of position—can take their place with confidence at any of the St Moritz rinks. To enjoy this ancient sport it is only necessary to follow the advice of the Sanquhar Society in 1776:

> If you'd be a curler keen,
> Stand right, look even,
> Sole well, shoot straight,
> And sweep clean.

6

The Cresta and the Bob

Everyone is fascinated by the Cresta run. Why has no one celebrated it in prose or verse? It might have been done by Hemingway, who delighted in the slightly more gory ordeals in the bull-ring; by Scott Fitzgerald; in a more restrained English manner in a chapter by Anthony Powell; or in an illustrated pastiche by Osbert Lancaster. But it mesmerises everyone— riders who get up early in the morning to try their skill on the icy run; spectators who are prepared to forgo their *café complet* in bed in order to face the cold before the sun appears over the southern peaks; and even those who have never been to St Moritz but who are appalled by its test of nerve and judgment. The fame of the present champions has spread throughout Europe: they are nerveless athletes with euphonious names like Hans Kuderli, Fischbacher, Ciparisso and, the greatest of all, the Italian Nino Bibbia, the complete epitome of the happy rider. (Bliss was it in that dawn to be alive, but on the Cresta very heaven.) The English, too, have always been prominent among the riders, including that great individualist Lord Brabazon of Tara who made his own mark on the Cresta, as on all other forms of locomotion he touched, from aircraft to automobiles, and Colin Mitchell who takes time off from the Royal Air Force to compete on his own terms with the Homeric Bibbia. The Cresta has its own élite, mystique, and a long list of *mutilés*.

No one has successfully explained the reason for the continuing fascination of what remains a fairly juvenile sport consisting basically of sliding down a hillside, lying on one's stomach, on a small metal frame like a tin tray. Very probably it is the vestigial adolescent aspect that provides the enduring attraction. To elevate the supreme pleasure of youthful sledging to the status of a serious sport demanding world attention is quite an achievement. Peter Badrutt saw this as long ago as 1894 when, addressing the St Moritz Tobogganing Club, he said:

> We Swiss looked upon tobogganing as a fitting amusement for children, until you Englishmen came among us and made of it a sport for men; now you have gone still further —you have made that sport an art.

There is also a whiff of danger to whet the appetite. A painful crash is always a possibility ('Michael will not be coming to the King's Club tonight') and it is not necessary to be thrown out of the trench which forms the run to break a limb— a collision with the wall can have the same painful effect—and it is clear to everyone that the rider puts himself at risk when he sets off through the gate.

This is a sport where skill and experience count and where the novices have to be segregated, but, while the main prizes often go to the young, less agile competitors can still hurl their more portly forms down the run in the veterans' competitions. Nor should it be forgotten that there is something bizarre about a game where the participants are advised not to shave beforehand lest they get frostbite, since their faces will be very, very near the ice as they hurtle downwards. This is the only social occasion when Anglo-Saxon morale is not impaired by a stubbly chin.

The main field of battle lies just to the north of the road from St Moritz to Celerina and for part of its length, particularly at the finish, it runs parallel to the bob run on the south side of the road. It is not really very easy to find (the more unusual sports from real tennis to falconry are all practised in decent privacy). There are no direction posts and there are many more obvious features to be recognised from a distance than a winding trench in the snow. But the run can be detected from the canvas screens put up to prevent melting in the Engadine sun, the unusual shape of the clubhouse, the confident calls on the loud-hailer, and the frozen breath of the loyal crowds at Junction, Battledore and Shuttlecock. Officially the run measures precisely 1346 yds and the difference in altitude between the start and the finish is 515 ft., although the run itself varies slightly from year to year. It is usual to open by stages, allowing a longer course as there has been time for practice and as conditions improve. In December the run used to start from Stream Corner (slightly more than halfway), but the start is now from Junction, and by early February the whole run is open from Top. The last section adds sharply to the height of the drop; the conditions are suddenly more demanding; and the run looks considerably more formidable from Top (which is just above the Catholic Church of St Moritz-Dorf). There is not a great deal of difference between the original or early Victorian courses and the present one as regards length, altitude or the general contours, but the run is now much more icy and the ten banks are of more permanent construction.

The origins of the Cresta go back to the last century when John Addington Symonds is thought to have organised the first toboggan races between visitors and the local inhabitants. These took place down the ordinary post roads through the village on wooden frame sledges, indigenous to the Engadine, called 'schlittli'. The schlittli resembled present-day children's toboggans and were ridden in the sitting position. It was not long before it was realised that a head-on position, lying prone, gave more excitement and better control and racing became a real possibility. Next came a particular 'Swiss' type of toboggan and the wooden runners were replaced by iron ones; but, in turn, they were soon abandoned in favour of the 'America', or clipper-sled, which was equipped with advanced round steel-sprung runners. (The round runners reduced friction on the ice.) J. A. Bott discovered the advantage of using a sliding seat.

From this it was a simple piece of evolution to produce the steel skeleton now in use, and not the least of W. H. Bulpett's fame is to have introduced the skeleton to St Moritz. Since then H. E. Forster is credited with introducing (about 1896) grooves on the runners, and the frames are now more scientifically made of lighter materials.

The first Cresta run was measured out in 1884 by a trio comprising one of the Badrutt family, Peter, together with George Robertson from Australia, and an Englishman, Digby Jones. It would be enormously interesting to learn whether they knew what they were doing—creating a new sporting medium—but unfortunately no record of their (semi-frozen) thoughts as they paced down the first course has survived. A glass of grog at the Kulm may have fortified their resolve. In any event, racing started in 1885 and the St Moritz Tobogganing Club was formed two years later. The first committee consisted of the Duke of Grazioli, Major Dwyer and Messrs Bulpett and Barber. The Grand National race was so called to distinguish it from the International race at Davos, where tobogganing had been started earlier on the Buol run—and at the Klosters Road.

In the early days it was the custom to start each season by treading down the snow, packing it on the line of the track, smoothing it and then building up banks of earth to be covered with snow and ice. It is not wholly fanciful to compare the first icemen, tramping down the run with canvas wrapped round their heavy boots in order to provide a well-trodden path, with Napoleon's alleged device of sending cattle first over the Julier Pass to facilitate the passage of his troops through the snow. (This comparison first struck Theodore White, one of the early secretaries of the Tobogganing Club.) The next stage was to beat the tramped-down surface with great wooden shovels. Taking the whole length of the run, this must have been a time-consuming and exhausting business. The main bends were then built up and the curves subjected to a series of tests to ensure that mathematically they were neither too oblique nor too acute.

It is of the first importance that the frame should be able to enter a curve in a straight line and emerge from it in another straight line, although possibly at right angles to the original course of direction. There must be nothing tangential; otherwise there would soon be a hole in the curved wall. After the trials, which would take some days but had to be completed against the clock since valuable racing time was being lost, the whole run was watered down so that it would freeze at night and provide a hard surface. In time it was realised that the banks were wearing away too fast from the constant knocking by the frames and it became the practice to depend more and more on ice proper instead of packed snow with a thin veneer of ice. While this makes the run faster and more uniform, it also makes it more rigid and more dangerous.

Bulpett, who possibly made the biggest contribution to the development of the Cresta run, always had doubts about icing the run in such a way that much higher speeds were produced. Although he planned the famous bends now known as Church Leap, Shuttlecock and the one near the end known as Bulpett's Corner which preserves his name, he greatly preferred skill to pace. But the temptation to go faster than the previous rider and to endorse anything that improved the speed of the run proved too great. For the first twenty-three years of its existence the Cresta run never saw a fatal accident, but there were two in 1907. Captain H. S. Pennell, VC, died from the injuries which he received after a fall in the hard snow, and soon afterwards Comte Jules de Bylandt, a highly expert rider, was killed on the run when he hit a plank of wood which had been left lying across the track. Stern precautions are taken nowadays to ensure that the run is absolutely clear before anyone leaves Top or Junction.

The fall of 515 ft. in the course of the run produces overall a gradient of 1 in 8, and it has been calculated that it would be possible in a straight line to achieve a speed of 130 mph. Fortunately for the skin, limbs and nerves of the riders, however, this figure makes no allowance for friction or for the slowing down necessary to navigate the bends, and the maximum speed reached is about 80 mph. The great Bibbia has been timed as reaching 88 mph. Steering is now done by change of balance and by fearsome-looking spikes worn on the toecaps instead of by pegs held in each hand. It is not easy to apply the spikes accurately enough to ensure the proper braking effect when it is needed and skill is required in altering the disposition of the rider's body on the frame to ensure the right balance when entering or leaving the bends. The straights should, in the classical manner, be ridden with the weight as far forward on the frame as possible. The rakes on the boots should not be used on the straights, otherwise speed is lost; the proper correction should be made by moving the head and shoulders.

Incidentally, the smart Alpine costume worn by riders today has, in contrast to most other sports, developed in such a way as to make it thicker and afford greater protection than in the past. Last century, Harry Gibson's view was that:

> The Eton boating-cap makes an excellent headgear, as it clings closely to the head and is not easily affected by the wind.

Today the crash-helmet, together with the heavy pullovers, knickerbockers and padding on the shoulders, elbows and knees, combine to produce an ensemble which would not look out of place on an astronaut.

A run from Top is full both of hazard and mounting pressure as the speed of the frame accelerates. If the rider has started through the gate from Top when the bell sounds, his first problem is to negotiate Church Leap, Curzon, Thoma, then a long straight past the Junction Start and into Rise, then Battledore (both it and Shuttlecock were christened by Squire Bancroft) which turns at right angles. The rider must take Battledore firmly and quickly and a low entry is one of the main essentials in a successful run. If the rider goes too high he will go over the top with one of the nastiest drops in the course awaiting him. There is a very small margin of error since the banks of the Cresta are, diabolically, built not a centimetre higher than is necessary. If, however, he goes too low, the rider will not come out of Battledore straight enough to have a reasonable chance at Shuttlecock which lies immediately after-wards and turns back through 90 degrees.

Shuttlecock is where the crowd gathers because that is where most riders come to grief—and obligingly do so in the most appealing fashion, flying straight through the air. But while much sadistic delight can be found in watching the discomfited rider thrown on to the snow outside the bank, fortunately serious accidents are few. Riders are advised to roll themselves up in a ball if they are thrown out of the run in order to reduce the shock on falling, and to push the skeleton away.

By Stream Corner the rider has done 700 yds. and is over half-way. Next comes the treacherous straight when the speed of the frame will increase with great rapidity; round Bulpett's Corner with growing confidence; then the very fast right-handed Charybdis, dropping to the Cresta Leap and through the timing contact. Finally, uphill to the Finish. The rider comes to rest, breathless and snowy, but with a sense of achievement which no other sport will provide. The timing devices are now so refined that it will be only a matter of seconds before he learns whether he has done a good time or must face the derision of his colleagues. Then there is the ride back in the lorry to the starting point; an interesting ride where the sense of accomplishment is tempered, possibly, by some self-criticism at going too early, or late, into a particular bend, and determina-tion to do a second or so better the next time, and a studied indifference to all spectators on the way.

Cresta running is now a highly sophisticated sport. The village runs of the early days, with the famous original bends (which must have been exceedingly perilous to pedestrians) known as Caspar's Corner and Belvedere, and the Lake Run from the Kulm down the footpath to the Beau Rivage and then to the lake, which allowed racing two abreast, are now no more. Instead, the Cresta run is electronically controlled and no time is lost between runs and the imperative tones of the umpire's voice relayed to everyone through the amplifying system. In the last ten years a well designed and highly individual clubhouse has been built and the elevated accommodation gives members a bird's-eye view of much of the course. This is one of the last modish, totally irrational, but—as a rule—utterly harmless, pastimes.

The connection with the Badrutt family is preserved in the frequent sorties which Cresta riders make to the Kulm Hotel where they often have their quarters. The Kulm, conveniently near to the run, is punctilious in publishing the times accomplished during the day's races and in posting the arrangements for the next day, and much of the Cresta business is conducted in the convivial atmosphere of the Sunny Bar. There too, lubricated by champagne cocktails, the sweepstake for the Fairchilds McCarthy Cup is held in January along with the procedures on other famous trophies. Those who study the handicaps and watch the performance in the early mornings of practice can make a good killing by buying a share in one of the less favoured riders who happens to be in form. But even allowing for the competitions and the wagering on the Grand National, the Curzon and the Fairchilds McCarthy, this is not really what it is all about. Panache, skill and danger—the whole purpose of the exercise is to test the nerves against the ice and see how fast it is possible to travel in safety, or, at least, near safety.

When the tired Cresta runner makes his way back to the village to pass the time of day with Bibbia and his wife (and possibly buy some bünderfleisch or a bottle of kirsch at his delicatessen store) he finds in Bibbia's suave grin a reflection of years of excitement. He will have no difficulty in matching the stories of incredible deeds by skiers who have just come down from Piz Nair, Diavolezza or Corvatsch. But he will know that he is a true disciple of St Mauritius. He will know too that, although racing on the Cresta is keener (and a shade more serious) than ever before, he still preserves the spirit of the

Oh, no!

Piz Morteratsch

Corviglia

Summer ski-ing at Corvatsch

Piz Nair summit and the Goat

The Ski Marathon: 1970: 4000 starters

Past the post

Leap out of the landscape

Trotting: A strange art
form on the snow

Ski-kijöring in the sun

A peaceful view from Chantarella

Start of the Regatta, 1970

Evening rise on Lake Champfer

The summer idyll: Princess Ira von Furstenberg with her children

The peaks in summer:
from left to right, Julier,
Roseg, Bernina and
Morteratsch

From Muottas Muragl to the
Roseg Valley and Piz Palu

Rocking-Horse Race in 1894. In the words of Harry Gibson, one of the two contestants, the rules were:

> Catchweights, the riders to be dressed in full hunting kit— viz. top hats, red coats, leathers, tops, and spurs. Both competitors to be mounted upon rocking-horses, which should be fitted with steel runners.

In the great sporting public at large there is much understandable confusion between the Cresta run and the bob run and few who have not been to St Moritz fully realise that they are not the same thing and that the runs, the equipment used and the technique practised are all utterly different. Basically, the Cresta rider gets up early in the morning, puts on his Martian gear and carries his frame to the starting point. There he stands in comparative isolation, beating his hands and stamping his feet to keep his circulation going. When the rider in front of him has either completed his course or been swept off the run, the signal comes for him to start. He throws himself on to the skeleton and glides away in a prone position with his nose a millimetre away from the frozen surface which he traverses with growing speed.

Nothing annoys the Cresta rider or the bob runner more than to find that a description of his heroic activities has not been understood and that his audience thinks that the Cresta rider is describing his performance on the bob, or vice versa. The bob runner is a team man and his activities are carried out either with a single partner (the two-man boblet) or with three others in the bobsleigh proper. The bobber and his mates manhandle the bob itself to the starting point—there is a primitive winch for dragging it up from the lorry in the car park. There is much rocking of the bob to and fro to ensure that the metal runners are clear and that the start (a highly important part of the run) will be a fast one. After this rhythmic process is thought to have gone on long enough the two middle men will join the driver in the bob, leaving only the brakeman to give it a final push, running as hard as he can for twenty yards

G

or so before leaping on to the frame as it gathers speed down
the run. (If he fails to get on, the rest of the team will soon
realise that they have no brake and that they are on their own.)
It is essentially a combined exercise.

These differences in technique are very apparent in the
temperament and outlook of the athletes who affect either the
Cresta or the bob. There are those who have been known to
attempt both, but seldom did they do so with anything like
equal concentration. A Cresta rider, for example, might try to
get a run on a bob on an afternoon when his serious morning
business on the Cresta is complete and the run is closed for the
day. He will be politely welcomed by the bobbers, but it will be
apparent that he is intent on relaxation. The Cresta rider can be
distinguished by the distant far-away look in his eye (not
caused, as has been suggested, by excessive gin). He says
remarkably little in the clubhouse before his run—or, for that
matter, over breakfast in his hotel—and he takes some time to
readjust himself to normal existence when his ride is over. He
is recognised by all as a dedicated man.

The bob runner, as one would expect from the nature of
the task which he has set himself, is more extrovert and
gregarious. Like members of rowing eights, bob teams are accustomed to wander about St Moritz together as though continued
proximity would enable them to grow common sinews which
would help them when they were competing. This is scarcely
surprising since their survival on the run depends on their
ability to maintain a uniform balance and keep their crash-
helmets perfectly in line as they gather speed down the run.
They live in an atmosphere which can best be described as
being one of mutual understanding, as thoughtful of each other
as they are gently contemptuous of non-bobbers.

Their clubhouse, surrounded by bobs, camp followers and
lorry drivers bringing the bobs back from the bottom of the run,
is a somewhat primitive erection. Its main feature is a wooden
panelled bar whose walls are covered with the autographed
photographs of past champions, interlaced with suitable graffiti.

It is a smokier, noisier and much more friendly place than the austere concrete of the Cresta clubhouse. Recurring rounds of refreshment are punctuated by the bell which summons the next team to start on its way down the run. Before long the time done by the previous bob will be announced over the loud-hailer to be greeted by ribald, patronising or critical cheers as the performance warrants. For bobbers and spectators alike it is always a great deal warmer and cosier inside the bar than at the lonely top of the run situated on an eminence in Badrutt's Park. There remains one other point of comparison. It is a matter of unresolved dispute whether the female companions who succour their heroes from the bob run are more alluring than the Cresta girls who cluster round Shuttlecock. But this contest will be continued later in the day in the Cresta bar at Steffani's or the King's Club at the Palace.

To make confusion worse confounded, the affairs of bobsleighers were originally watched over by the St Moritz Tobogganing Club (which ran, and still runs, the Cresta). The break came when, at the time when Cresta riders were still in the course of developing their frames from the original prototype of the old Swiss schlittli, an American (Mr S. Whitney) produced a 'bob sled' which was a longer and apparently more cumbrous machine composed of two frames of the 'pig-sticker' type joined together. There was a longer frame to lean on and in front of it a shorter one which could be used for steering. The two were connected by a board which worked upon swivels for steering round corners. This was first tried at Davos and it was not long before the bob sled had begun to prove its superiority over the 'America' which had emerged from the schlittli. Bobsled runners attempted to compete in the International Race at Davos on the ground that it was open to any class of machine, but the 'bob sled, bobsleigh, or double-Ripper' was declared to be illegal and ineligible to compete in the international event. The bobsleighers then, in the words of Harry Gibson, took themselves off to 'the lighter paths of the sport'. Not for them the calculated precision of the Cresta run. In time it was thought that there were enough bobbers with an interest in the sport to form a club to supervise their own activities and at the beginning of the 1898 season the St Moritz Bobsleigh Club was formed—the oldest bobsleigh club in the world.

The first official bobsleigh race promoted by the new club was held on 5th January 1898. The winner was a bobsleigh with the unsuitable name of 'Alligator', steered by Mr G. St Aubyn, and the race took place on the Cresta road from St Moritz down to the village of Cresta. Bobsleighing soon became so popular and fleets of bobs coursing down the main road reached such proportions that even in those days of light traffic the need for a separate run could no longer be overlooked. After a number of detailed surveys, which aimed to please bobbers, spectators and hoteliers alike, Mr James Chambers' plan was thought to be the best, and the run, which has remained ever since on very much the same line, was opened in the 1903–4 season. The Badrutt family, active as always in anything which furthered the tourist welfare of St Moritz, provided a loan to cover the capital cost involved.

Unlike the Cresta, the St Moritz bob run cannot claim to be unique and there are several comparable ones in other European resorts—mostly built like those at Cortina d'Ampezzo and the disastrous one at Alpe D'Huez on the occasion of the Winter Olympics. The St Moritz run is, however, the oldest and, although it is the slowest, it is still the most difficult and the fairest for competitors. An element of danger is inescapable in bobbing. On a black day in February 1968 twenty-eight went to hospital, but the St Moritz run is so constructed that really serious accidents have not been as numerous as might be expected. The Cortina run might be slightly more spectacular, and I do not forget walking its length during the summer with the friendly Italian expert, Renato Menaiggo, who argued with characteristic eloquence that the bends had been constructed with geometric precision. There is a precipitous straight in the middle of the Cortina run which makes it difficult for the true bobber without either braking or unnecessary risk. The

spate of accidents in the competitions throughout Europe in the
1970 season emphasised once again the fine balance between
danger, triumph and disaster.

Like all international bob runs, the St Moritz one is about a
mile in length and has three large banked bends. The International Federation actually prescribes 1600 metres and sixteen
bends in all. The run begins at a height (increased in recent
years) in Badrutt's Park and twists and turns through a total
drop of nearly 400 ft. till it ends on a slight ascent just outside
the village of Celerina.

A well-known English driver, who has just retired after
splitting his crash-helmet, but, fortunately, not his skull,
describes driving a two-man boblet through the bends:

> First, I check the sled to make certain that all the bolts are
> tight; that the steering is correct; and that nothing has
> frozen up. Then I tease the brakeman to ensure that he
> will really flex his muscles to give us a good start. We begin
> to rock the sled backwards and forwards. One . . . two . . .
> three . . . go. We run as though fired from a gun; I jump in
> and collect the rope handles. I feel the brakeman tap my
> back which tells me that he is with me. I try to steer
> straight, moving the ropes as little as possible. We gather
> speed. We go into Wall late . . . I take it as smoothly as
> possible . . . I have not lost much time. Snake already. Now
> I must get in early and keep low at Sunny. Steady . . . we
> are skidding in Nash. The brakeman shouts something
> encouraging and I begin to be obsessed by the sight of a
> small screw in the cowling. The big bend on Horseshoe
> comes and goes . . . I am early into Telephone . . . early
> into Shamrock . . . and we are through Dyke. Now for the
> final concentration at Bridge. I feel the wind as we whistle
> into the straight at 80 mph. I will hold steady and try not
> to hit the sides . . . take Leap late . . . and we are through
> like a flash. A natural line in Portago and past the timing
> contact. The brakeman brakes and we slow to a stop.

The bob itself was originally a sledge with two swivelling front runners. Then it was a simple metal frame where the front runners were steered by pulling on ropes. Now the bob has a scientifically designed metal superstructure which reduces wind resistance. For a time a steering wheel was used, but ropes are now once again preferred for giving a faster touch and better balance. A great deal of research has gone into the design of bobs —steering, suspension, and streamlining—and the room for further development is possibly small. In 1965 the Americans arrived in Europe with two sleds built by General Motors. They were too fast to be manageable and the wrecked skeletons were soon shipped back to Detroit. The RAF, whose team usually appears at St Moritz, have made their own contribution and tried to see whether applied aeronautics has anything to offer. But bobbers are not secretive about their equipment; they are not chary about using each other's, and are very willing to pool experience. There was, for example, the famous occasion when the great Italian bobber Eugenio Monti, nine times world champion, loaned a vital part of the bob axle to his nearest English rivals, Nash and Dixon, in the concluding stage of the 1964 Winter Olympics at Igls—which the Englishmen subsequently won.

The sense of exhilaration derived from bobbing is basically very like the feeling of achievement which the Cresta rider feels when he has finished his course: but the bob is heavier and bobbing is harder work. The novice, even if he remembers not to hold on as tightly as he can throughout the course (this will lead to cramp), will certainly have stiff forearms and stiff neck muscles the next day as the unwelcome result of too tight tenacity. The core of the bobber's approach is the teamwork involved. One head out of line and time will be lost; one bobber out of balance and the bob will be upset: all this in less than a minute and a half.

The English invented, and for long periods monopolised, the Cresta. Bobbing is a much more international sport and the St Moritz run is always populated by teams from most European countries. The Germans, the Austrians, the Italians and the Swiss are all keen competitors. (Before the 1914 war the Crown Prince of Germany was Honorary President of the St Moritz Bobsleigh Club and acquired great skill as a driver.) After the last war, however, Mr Hubert Martineau did more than anyone else to revive the prosperity of the St Moritz Club and Nash and Dixon have been among the most prominent runners. For the time being, the fortunes of English competitors on the track are somewhat in decline, although they are still welcomed under the genial Presidency of Gunther Sachs. And a salute must be made to Franz Kapus, who won the 1956 Olympic bobbing title and is now responsible for building up the track every year.

An envoi for those who want to attempt these recondite sports for the first time. All Cresta riders have to start from scratch, as do very many bobbers. Few have the opportunity to practise except in the short space of an annual winter holiday. The clubs will receive you and ensure that you get a chance, even though the bobbers are putting themselves at risk by including a novice in the team. With a little prudence all will be well and you will be able to claim the privileges—the table reserved for bobbers at the Chesa Veglia or the genial rites at the Cresta and Sunny Bars—which are much prized by those who have completed the course.

7

Ski-ing

Ski-ing is now the prime winter sport and proficiency on the piste is a peremptory requirement, both athletic and social, for anyone who wants 'to shine in the high aesthetic line, as a man of culture rare'. But, in retrosepct, the odd thing is that it took such an exceptionally long time for anyone in Central Europe to start on skis. There was nothing new about traversing the snow-fields—on snow-shoes like the Eskimos, on sleds like the Finns or on pulkas like the Lapps—and these practices had been followed for centuries. The first recorded mention of anything which can be recognised as ski-ing is probably in a book written in 1689 by an Austrian called Valvasor which made it clear that the Austrians in some of the provinces near the Adriatic were already expert ski-runners. But there was still to be a long winter before ski-ing emerged with any popularity in Europe, and Sir Arnold Lunn, with his keen sense of history, was puzzled to note that when he began to ski in 1898 it was still the sport of a few eccentrics. By then, however, the message was being learned very quickly and the spread of ski-ing outside Scandinavia accelerated throughout the last decade or so of the nineteenth century and the first of this century. Ski-ing first appeared in Switzerland, not in one of the fashionable centres, not in St Moritz or Zermatt or Davos or Arosa. Lunn inclines to the view that the first expert ski-runner in Switzerland was probably the Norwegian O. Kjelsberg, who introduced ski-ing into Winterthur in 1889. The Swiss themselves award the palm to the small cantonal capital of Glarus at the foot of the Glärnisch in the eastern part of Switzerland. It is said that a young inhabitant of Glarus, Christoph Iselin, was so excited by reading Nansen's *On Snowshoes through Greenland* that he fashioned a pair of ski-like boards and started his descent through the snow. It is, in any event, true that the first ski club was formed in Glarus in 1893 and eleven years later it acted as godfather to the Swiss Ski Association.

The English were soon involved, as with all winter sports in their infancy. Ruskin might sneer at his fellow countrymen hurling themselves down the slopes, but there was no doubt that this was to be the latest—and the strongest—manifestation of the Anglo-Saxons' love of the Alps. In 1888 an Englishman, Colonel Napier, brought a pair of skis to Davos, and the ski-ing possibilities and the attendant hazards attracted immediate attention, particularly from the English visitors. Three years later Gerald Fox started ski-ing in Grindelwald and in 1894 Sir Arthur Conan Doyle, with a party of friends and guides, crossed the Mayenfelder Furka from Davos to Arosa. This was the first Anglo-Saxon ski-ing sortie and was only beaten by a year to be the first recorded ski expedition in the Alps—the crossing of the Pragel Pass by a Swiss party led by Iselin. Conan Doyle published an amusing account of the outcome in the *Strand* magazine, and ended with a remarkable prophecy that hundreds of Englishmen would soon come to ski in Switzerland in March and April. In this, as in many other matters, Conan Doyle demonstrated his gift of second sight. The great E. C. Richardson, who is generally recognised as the father of British ski-ing, first visited Davos in 1901 and founded the Ski Club of Great Britain two years later. From then on the English claimed ski-ing as their own.

Ski-ing in Switzerland, as in all areas where it is practised to any great extent, is both an organised and an individual sport. It has to be organised nowadays because of the very number of skiers involved and the need for someone with authority to take charge of the funiculars, chair-lifts, ski-tows and all the other mechanised aids that carry out the Sisyphean task of transporting skiers 'all day for ever, up and down the hill'. Someone also has to be responsible for general safety, for seeing that the foolhardy and inexpert are discouraged from leaving the well-tried routes, for watching the condition of the snow and for guarding against the unwary diversion which might start an avalanche. The days of individual pioneers and enthusiasts who provided the earliest facilities are past and this is now a task for syndicates or State intervention. Lastly, an organisation is required to run the competitive events, approve standards, and award the badges and all the Alpine insignia which keen skiers greatly covet and love to tattoo on their anoraks. We come to racing later.

But the fundamental attraction of ski-ing as a sport is the unusual opportunity which it provides for the expression of individuality. The skier on his own challenges the elements and for a time the laws of gravity. Terrestrial ties are cast aside as the skier glides improbably down the sheer edge of the landscape at ever-increasing speed. There are many other attractions— the growing excitement of buckling on unfamiliar equipment, the abrasive bonhomie of fellow skiers on the climb to the top of the run and the final adjustment of gear before starting downhill. But no part of the drill matches the sense of individual challenge and compared to this only the vista, the breathtaking prospect which stretches before the skier at the summit, has any real significance.

There are three aspects of the art form which for our purpose need only the lightest touch with an alpenstock: mountaineering, jumping and racing. Mountaineering, which can be combined with some forms of ski-ing and leading to ski journeys on the highest ridges, has never been much practised at St Moritz or the surrounding area, possibly because the St Moritz peaks have a neat, engraved-like quality and are not constructed on the formidable scale which attracts the mountaineer. Ski-jumping is a form of lunacy reserved for Icareans and we have noted their appearance at St Moritz for the Olympic Games in the Twenties and Thirties chapter.

There is racing every year during the winter season at St Moritz and it is often not long before the young and agile, as soon as they have won their badges, are tempted by the thrill of the downhill run or the stern test imposed by the slalom. Racing itself provides the supreme test of skill and nerve. There are few fatal, but many serious, accidents. The racer must be prepared to reach a speed of at least 60 mph, with the possibility of falling head first. (80 mph has been recorded at St Moritz.) Peter Lunn found in racing the unique mixture of the sensual pleasure to be derived from mere speed and the intellectual pleasure of imposing one's will on a sometimes unwilling set of muscles. He recalls the sense of isolation that the racer feels on the top slopes where few spectators go—a feeling which is much keener than is aroused even by the roar of friendly encouragement near the end of the run. Lunn found that the most exciting days of racing were during the practice runs when all the unusual slopes, or bumps, or the best line to be taken, were studied metre by metre by all the expert runners who were to take part in the race. In the race itself most of the crowd would not be able to appreciate the finer points, but they would be closely scrutinised by fellow racers during training.

Sir Arnold Lunn has an inalienable right to be regarded as the originator of competitive ski-ing as it is known today. He was alone responsible for obtaining international recognition for both the downhill and slalom races as an addition to the Scandinavian langlaf, but it took him until 1930 to achieve his objective. The slalom was Sir Arnold's particular love and, not surprisingly, the first slalom races were held at Mürren, with which the Lunn family were always associated. Sir Arnold stressed that the slalom provided a test which was both physical and mental and, in his view, 500 ft. of slalom racing was more exhausting than 2000 ft. downhill. The slalom racer, for example, can never let himself go all out; he must retain something in reserve. Unlike the downhill racer, he is in full view of the crowd, and one mistake is much more difficult to recover than in downhill racing.

Coming from a country which has no Alpine heights, the English have done remarkably well in ski-racing, and it is no coincidence that the three great racing clubs—the Kandahar, the Downhill Only and Marden's—which were founded in the 1920s and based respectively on Mürren, Wengen and Davos, are all of English origin. These clubs have exercised a profound and continuing influence on Alpine ski-ing, and Marden's Ski Club, with its main homes at Davos and Klosters, has promoted racing throughout the Grisons since 1928. Almost without exception, the most successful British racers have been members of one of these clubs. It would appear that the prestige attached to membership, together with some of the elements of discipline which the clubs impose, has an indefinable, but beneficial, effect on ski-ing technique.

The British National Men's and Women's teams have frequently trained at St Moritz at the beginning of the racing season, and the British Army have held their championships at St Moritz for many years, the Duke of Kent being prominent among the competitors. A favourite, but irrelevant, recollection of one Army Championship relates to a general's wife staying in an hotel where the heating had temporarily failed. She provided a hungry picture as she sat in the dining-room obstinately clutching the hot-plate to her chest in order to keep warm, and declining to leave until she had received her rations.

The Commonwealth Winter Games have been held at St Moritz every four years since their inception in 1958, the last occasion being in December 1970. Both the Army Championships and the Commonwealth Games have received very lively co-operation, which they are very ready to recognise, from the St Moritz Kurverein and the local racing organisation. St Moritz's adaptability and experience in ski-racing were demonstrated recently by the successful way in which it was able to take over at very short notice the organisation of the famous Lauberhorn Race in January 1971 when lack of snow at Wengen, its normal venue, had threatened cancellation. The racing connection—which led the Aga Khan, at one time a

British National racer, to acquire his own chalet at St Moritz—preserves the earlier kinship between St Moritzers and Anglo-Saxon enthusiasts. St Moritz has since been selected as host for the World Alpine Ski Championships in 1974.

Although there has been racing, and good racing, at St Moritz every year, its primacy as a ski resort does not really depend on the racing that takes place there. This is no new development. Captain Marden, who founded the Grisons (now Marden's) Club, recalled that:

> The Grisons has been the home of those who might perhaps be called 'the gentlemen of the mountains', those genial souls who love the snow and the sun and who ski for pleasure.

St Moritz ski-ing is for fun and for this purpose there are no better slopes than the great massif to the north of the village, from Chantarella and Suvretta to Piz Nair. If a St Moritzer were asked to make an invidious comparison with other ski-ing resorts he would admit that there were attractions at St Anton. He would also recognise, if pressed, that St Moritz did not have a run of the apparently interminable length of the Parsenn at Davos. He might even admit that, late in the season, good ski-ing was still to be had at the extreme heights of Obergurgl. But he would not be worried that St Moritz would maintain its place in the forefront. St Moritz has remained unshaken by the formidable expansion of ski-ing in the French Alps and elsewhere. It is true that at Val d'Isère the descents are more acute, and this is probably the place for sharpening up one's racing technique. Courchevel, with its enormous single massif, its complex of runs through the Trois Vallées and its latticework of ski-tows, probably provides more ski-ing within easy reach and more continuous runs than any other resort, but, compared with St Moritz, it is strangely brash and lacks charm.

St Moritz ski-ing is not only for fun, it is for everyone, and the great variety of mechanical aids ensures that everyone who skis can have as much downhill ski-ing (and of the appropriate standard) as he wants. Many of the runs are similar in character, with their wide pistes which are kept in excellent condition, but it is not long before the skier can tell by instinct exactly which run he is traversing. This is one of the oddities of ski-ing: everyone has a particular run at Zermatt or Verbier or St Moritz where—although to the uninformed it may seem just like any other piste—he feels most at home. St Moritz is lucky in having four major ski areas within reach. These include the famous runs known by the names of their areas—Corviglia-Piz Nair, above St Moritz itself; Marguns-Trais Fluors, above Celerina; Corvatsch, on the other side of the valley opposite St Moritz; and Pontresina-Diavolezza. The first two of these areas are contiguous and the moderately expert skier can cover the whole of the slopes from Suvretta to Marguns, the main division being a deep cleft, known as the Gully, which runs down from Munt da San Murezzan between the Corviglia Bahn and the Salastrains lift.

The starting point for most skiers at St Moritz is the funicular from Schoolhouse Square in the centre of St Moritz-Dorf. The funicular goes first to Chantarella and stops near the spacious hotel where the less active are sunning themselves. But this is, meanwhile, of no interest to the skier. A short climb to start the circulation moving, and the beginners' playground of Salastrains and Alp Giop are reached. From Salastrains a lift climbs up the Alp Giop and serves the well-worn slopes, much populated by the ski instructors and their obedient, attendant classes in the painful throes of learning the first mysteries. Despite their height (7218 ft. at the summit), these are essentially nursery slopes although they are also used for slalom races.

A longer lift from Salastrains also rises to the Munt da San Murezzan which is on the Piz Nair plateau itself (8858 ft.). If, however, the skier has not left the funicular at Chantarella he will be taken up to Corviglia, which is the hub of St Moritz ski-ing. From there you can ski to Salastrains, Chantarella or Marguns. This is the highest point usually reached by non-

skiers intent on the more sybaritic delights of the Corviglia
Club. The flags of all nations surround the club, and even the
non-skiers are easily assured that they are absorbing an international ski-ing atmosphere. A sun-tan acquired in a deck-chair
is not easily distinguishable from one more painfully and ener-
getically earned by hours on the piste.

From Corviglia, however, set as it is on the junction of the
Celerina lift system and on the edge of the Piz Nair plateau
below the peak of Piz Nair itself, the dedicated skier will start
off for higher things. From Corviglia rises the cable-car to Piz
Nair with a steady climb over its eight minutes' run. It is only
after leaving Corviglia that the skier feels that he has entered the
remote area where those who are expert on skis will enjoy themselves. The sense of isolation grows with the climb. St Moritz
itself is no longer visible, and dismounting from the ski-lift at
the summit brings an unmistakably sharp air of adventure.
Here the air smells of snow. The restaurant at the end of the
ski-lift, the famous St Moritz goat statue, and the facetious
direction posts pointing to distant places, even outside Europe,
all seem irrelevant. All the most romantic ski runs are now at
the skier's feet. Heights, scenery, good powder snow and pistes
which will not necessarily impose too severe a test on the
moderate skier: all these now lie ahead, and they are seldom
found in the same place.

Starting from the top of Piz Nair, the skier has much ski-ing
before him. As he descends, he can ski over the whole of the
large massif on the south-facing slopes down from Corviglia,
and end in the Champfer–Suvretta–St Moritz valley. The runs,
which interweave with a basket-like pattern, are clearly named
and signposted, and there is no excuse for missing the poles.

For those who want a change it is possible to ski from Corviglia northwards down the northern side of the main Piz Nair–
Celerina route on the slopes that lead down to Marguns. There
are two ski-lifts which link the main Celerina and St Moritz ski
areas: one from Marguns to Corviglia and the other from
Marguns to near the top of the Piz Nair plateau.

The main runs in the area are sufficiently different to merit a more detailed description. Taken in order, they start with the *Standard-Salastrains* run (2 km.). This is a wide slope from Corviglia, not too sharp a descent, but—as though to prove it is not always funny—it soon takes the form of a rather weary traverse path which can become exposed and icy and is not particularly welcoming for beginners. The run then makes for the Gully, which at this height is still shallow before the Salastrains lift (where there is an SOS telephone, fortunately used only infrequently). It then continues by the Chinese Garden to Alp Giop and down the Signal run to Salastrains.

The *Race* run (1·9 km.), from the top of the Salastrains drag-lift, starts towards Suvretta. There is a good schuss down and up, followed by a steeper one; then a variety of choices—through the Chinese Garden to Alp Giop and down to the village or across to Suvretta. The act of selection makes the skier feel he is master of his fate—until he loses balance going too fast.

The *Akademiker* run (1·5 km.). Some style is needed for this fast run which is really for good skiers. Novices will find that it exposes any deficiencies in their technique. From Corviglia, it starts down the Standard run, crosses the Gully near the Salastrains drag-lift and turns left on an interesting schuss. On the edge of the Gully there is a cat-walk path (not for everyone), and then the piste retraces across the lift and follows down an easy slope to Salastrains.

The *Zwetschga* run (1·4 km.) resembles the Akademiker run but lies on the other side of the Gully. A gentle slope descends into a single, short, steep piste leading to an easy schuss near the traverse path at Standard. This is a run much enjoyed by those whose ski-ing technique is adequate to the demands. A successful accomplishment of the Zwetschga and the skier begins to nourish delusions of grandeur, stand himself an extra gluhwein, and make himself generally intolerable to the rest of his party.

The *Opel* run (1·3 km.), a short adventure run, is mainly for extroverts: it lies next to the funicular railway. Expe-

rienced performers who are prepared to risk a spectacular fall
in full view of passengers on the funicular will enjoy the
challenge, safe in the knowledge that skiers all look sadly alike
when they start to fall, and identical when they are upended.
St Moritzers particularly favour this run in spring-snow conditions early in March. The piste ends by crossing the railway to
join the Zwetschga, thereafter to Salastrains or Chantarolla.

The *Nater* run (1·5 km.) is sometimes referred to as the poor
man's Opel, of which it is a simplified and much gentler version.
It starts to the left of the Corviglia Club and runs down a
moderate decline into a saucer, turning on to the wide slopes
below Opel.

The *Olympic* run (2·0 km.) is one of the most popular and in
many ways is the most interesting run at St Moritz. It starts,
as does the Nater run, beside the Corviglia Club, but soon skis
straight into a saddle beyond which there is a dramatic bowl
with rocks on either side. A good slalom technique is needed to
take the run at speed, but there are few ski-ing experiences to
match the exhilaration of reaching the bottom through the trees
and finding the short gap which leads to the broad glade before
turning towards Chantarella.

The exciting and spectacular *Bushell* run (3·5 km.) from
Corviglia starts towards Marguns (which lies visible far below)
and after traversing the high ground drops down to join the
Celerina run. This is not for beginners since, although the run
is marked, there is no prepared piste.

Lastly in this area there is the *Celerina* run (3·0 km.) which
starts from Marguns, down the valley where it joins Bushell;
thereafter a path through the wood leads to the nursery slopes
at Celerina.

The ski-lifts from Suvretta House to the western edge of the
Piz Nair plateau complement the runs in our first area. The
sunny nursery slopes (and with their proximity to Suvretta
House, the gentle incline of their angle and the view down
towards Champfer, these must be the happiest nursery slopes
in the world) are crossed by a short beginner's drag-lift. From

H

the top of this the main system goes up to Randolins (7217 ft.) and thereafter to Plateau Nair (8559 ft.). The two main runs from the top are *Swing* to Randolins (1·5 km) and *Paradise* (2·0 km.). Swing is the ideal Suvretta piste for the medium-class skier, although it can sometimes be icy in the early morning. Starting to the west, round a shoulder there is a broad piste to give the skier confidence. This crosses to the lift in a pleasant schuss, doubles back and then curves away from the lift in a long traverse till it joins the Paradise run. Paradise is a longer run, farther west than Swing, and is often untracked. The piste, which is not wide, bears left throughout, curving and dropping gently without any problems, although sometimes icy until the sun has made itself felt. It joins up with Swing, and the combined run then leads back to Suvretta House. In short, this is the area for the first day of the holiday on skis. Not only the affluent guests at Suvretta come down from a morning on Swing and Paradise convinced that they have a future on the pistes. It is a run for everyone.

The first area is completed with a short look at the three great runs from Piz Nair itself. At the top of Piz Nair there are rocks and gullies and for all except the most experienced or foolhardy there are only three main pistes from the summit. First there is the gentlest of the three to *Champfer and Suvretta* (6·5 km.). After an initial descent down the traverse path the run turns west and glides down the slopes towards the Val Suvretta and Champfer itself. The Guinness Couloir, a lively run into the Suvretta Valley in spring-snow conditions, lies to the south of the main piste. Secondly there is the run to *Celerina* (7 km.) round the back of Piz Nair, down to Pass Schlattain, then a long, moderate descent by way of Marguns to Celerina; lengthy but not difficult. Finally there is the *Niarchos* run on the south face, which separates the men from the boys. The beginning of this run is only for experts, and anyone who attempts it must be well versed in advanced technique. Near the top station the run goes off at what seems to be an exceptionally sharp angle, only to descend even more acutely shortly after-

wards. After 1000 ft. or so of this exhilarating piste it levels out
north of the top station on the Suvretta system. This is the run
for someone who thinks he has made enough progress in his
weeks at St Moritz to try it as a test.

The second area—Celerina–Marguns–Trais Fluors—joins
the first one based on Corviglia to Suvretta. Cable-cars creep
up almost clandestinely from Celerina to the ski-ing area at
Marguns and at the Marguns junction two climb to the Corviglia area and one north-west to Trais Fluors. The area served
by this system, the Saluver Valley between Corviglia and the
ridge above the Trais Fluors top station, provides a vast south-
facing bowl. The pistes are, for the most part, easy and it is
also possible to ski at will without any apprehension. The skier
can enjoy the unusual pleasure of abandoning himself to the
snow. The three Trais Fluors runs are known as *Black* (1·5 km.),
Red (2·0 km.) and *Blue* (2·5 km.). The Black one, the easiest of
the three, provides excellent scope for experienced skiers.
Although it is fairly steep, there are no real difficulties and it has
the advantage that from Marguns the skier can study all the
possibilities for himself in advance. The wide slopes allow the
skier to choose whatever line he wishes. The Blue run is a
longer, easy one, seldom favoured by the larger crowds on the
neighbouring pistes; it gives a feeling of isolation and it is not
difficult, although on the narrow side. The Red one is more
difficult and has considerably more individuality. Descending
over a saddle, there is a traverse across a steep slope. Thereafter, a wider slope leads down to the valley itself. Those who
want something entirely different, and are prepared to climb on
foot (rather less than an hour) above the top station, can reach
an unusual glacier run down the Palud Marscha into the Val
Bevers, but this means being resigned to returning home by
train, which takes some of the icy gilt off the gingerbread.

St Moritz was for long criticised for having practically
nothing but south-facing slopes which offered ski-ing which
was, in most cases, of a fairly similar nature. The gradual build-
up of the Corvatsch ski area opposite St Moritz on the other

side of the valley has, however, changed all this. It has opened up a new dimension and has been the most exciting ski-ing development at St Moritz during the last decade. The Corvatsch formation, which runs from Piz Rosatsch and Piz Surlej, mounts up to Piz Corvatsch at the summit. To the west, the ridge then descends south of the lakes that lead to Maloja, and is divided from the Bernina one by the Roseg Valley. The views from the top provide an immediate reward for those who have made the ascent. Both the Matterhorn and Monte Rosa can be seen, as can the ice-falls of Piz Roseg and Piz Bernina.

Corvatsch is 6 km. to the south-west of St Moritz village beyond Silvaplana. Piz Corvatsch had for long been favoured as an excellent tour expedition from St Moritz, involving a climb of four or five hours; then it became increasingly popular for those who were prepared to take a helicopter ski-lift flight. But the decision, characteristic of those who have always kept St Moritz in the forefront, to develop a cableway to the summit has changed the whole pattern of ski-ing in the area. The first stage to the middle station was completed in March 1963, and the second one to the summit by the end of the same year. The cable-car runs from Surlej (6135 ft.) to Murtel (8868 ft.) and then to Corvatsch itself (10,820 ft.), and the majestic climb takes thirteen minutes in all. The north-facing runs, which greatly extend the local ski-ing season, form an admirable contrast to the more orderly southern snow-fields above St Moritz on the other side of the valley. In general they are keen enough to stretch the better skiers, but wide enough to be enjoyed even by an indifferent skier, and each of the runs, against their lonely background, has a virtue of its own. The whole scale of the landscape is impressive for its size alone. The wide expanse of undulating snow-fields of the Corvatsch glacier and the pistes down to Margun-Vegl are surprisingly different from the gentle valleys from Murtel to Surlej, and the last thousand feet or so provides pleasant ski-ing through the woods. As the Corvatsch area still involves what amounts to a day's expedition from St Moritz, it is relevant to note that, as might be expected, the thrifty Swiss have provided restaurants at Murtel and Corvatsch, a mountain hut of impeccable Alpine character at Fuorcla Surlej, and two more restaurants at the bottom.

There are nine north-facing runs, all of different character, depending on the altitude and whether they are below the tree line. To take just one example, the *Standard* run from the summit to Mandras (2 km.) descends from the start to the Corvatsch glacier, an extensive plateau which gradually becomes steeper and lasts for what seems a long time. There are various lines open to the skier to make his own choice, and eventually the run ends with a shallow valley down to Mandras where everyone can regain confidence and feel that his expedition was justified.

A quick look at the remaining runs nearby at Muottas Muragl, Pontresina and the Diavolezza area completes the conspectus. Muottas Muragl is conveniently situated between Pontresina, Celerina and Samaden. One of the oldest funiculars of all time still runs from Punt Muragl up to Muottas Muragl (8057 ft.). This run is improbably sited on a fringe of rock with chasm-like valleys on either side. It seems to point accusingly as Samaden Airport where the Engadine and Bernina valleys join. From the top of the run there is a vast distant prospect right down the lakes below St Moritz to Maloja and across the valley to the snow-face above the village. The atmosphere on the funicular and in the hotel at the top remains emphatically, although agreeably, Victorian. At night the lights in the Muottas Muragl Hotel ,viewed from Suvretta at the other end, seem to come from space: they appear to have no substance behind them. The view is the real attraction at Muottas Muragl and the ski-ing is not so good as elsewhere in St Moritz. It seems to catch just enough more sun than the rest of the valley to make the runs tend towards slush.

At Ponteresina there are convenient nursery slopes immediately behind the village, but they are too low for the snow to

survive much into March. There is a better run at Alp Languard in a sharp gully between the trees, but it, too, is only
skiable for a short time. The really exciting areas lie beyond
Pontresina at Diavolezza and Lagalb. The Diavolezza run lies
in open country astride the Bernina Pass which, in turn, is
dominated by the magnificent peaks of Piz Palu and Piz
Bernina. The cablecar to Diavolezza makes the climb to a
height of 9970 ft. carrying sixty persons a time, and taking ten
minutes to do it. Despite this, Diavolezza is often crowded and
the delays at the bottom can seem interminable. But when the
summit is reached the snow facing north is very good indeed.
Those who can avert their eyes from the piste will be intrigued
by the sight of the ice-falls on Piz Palu and Piz Bernina. There
is a single dominating run down *Diavolezza* itself which follows
the same line as the cableway. A long, gradual slope down to
Diavolezza Lake with a pleasant schuss across it, then to an
easy valley which makes even the most inefficient skier look like
a champion. This is one of the best runs in the whole of the St
Moritz area and is much beloved both by experts and by comparative tyros, but it can be very cold. The more adventurous
skiers can also try the *Morteratsch* run south of the Diavolezza
summit, with its unusual views of the glaciers and crevasses.
But there the piste is narrow; there is a cat-walk; and some
climbing is involved. It is not for the faint-hearted. Lastly there
is the much less crowded cableway from Curtinatsch to Lagalb
(9508 ft.). The pistes descend directly to the bottom of the
cable-car system and, since it faces north, the snow conditions
are normally excellent, although it can be too chilly for comfort.

In this snowy chapter we have said little about the incidentals
to a day's ski-ing—the delights of a sunny lunch in the open air
at Corviglia or the Zuberhut or the restaurant at the top of the
Suvretta lift; the heart-warming combination of sharp icy air,
warm sunshine and grog or gluhwein; or the descent to the
enticements of après ski. Instead, we have dwelt for the most
part on ski-ing proper, for it is on this that the St Moritzer will
say that the reputation of his village rests. Looking up from the

main square or from the curling rinks to the snow-fields above,
the ski-tows seem to creep relentlessly upwards like centipedes
in perpetual motion (except on the, happily, exceptional occa-
sions when power-cuts reduce them to immobility). And at a
distance the snow seems to be populated by a race of gnomes
or large insects scurrying improbably down the slopes. It is a
ski-ing world. The poet Robert Murray described the addiction
of St Andrews to golf as producing 'a city given over, soul and
body to a tyrannising game'. The same is true of St Moritz. If
skiers are not born wearing skis but grow them soon after birth,
surely their infancy should be spent here.

8

The Summer Idyll

There has been a surprising tendency in the last few decades to neglect St Moritz in the summer. This is particularly true of the Anglo-Saxons, and in July and August the platforms at Zürich station do not resound to the strains of coarse rugger during the ritual battles with the porters; at least, not with anything like the same frequency as they do in January and February. This is, to some extent, the penalty of success, since St Moritz has built itself up from a small Alpine village to be the leader of winter-sports centres. Those who are keenest to swarm down the pistes in the spring will tend to make for somewhere else in the summer. It is also partly due to the constricting English habit of assigning seasons for sports and then adhering to them with religious fervour. The most frightening admonition which the Fairy Queen in *Iolanthe* could give to the House of Lords was that they would not be released from Westminster before the August Bank Holiday:

> You will sit, if I see reason,
> In the grouse and salmon season.

Students of *il gran turismo*, however, see reason to believe that this may be only a temporary phase and that in future years St Moritz—not that it is in any way deserted in the summer— will ascend the summit of summer, as of winter, resorts. When the charred tourist returns from the last of many trips to the Costa Brava where, with his family, he has obediently grilled himself into an overdone tournedos, he will eventually realise that it was not much fun, and that the mountains and the lakes have very much more to offer.

St Moritz was a summer station long before Badrutt's bet brought the winter tourists, and the first European visitors began to congregate there primarily to take the waters, as we have described in the Pioneers chapter. Perhaps the legendary Mauritius was really the first summer visitor. Not much is known of him or his origins, and he does not stand high in the canon of saints, although the irreverent have been known to say that their practice of hagiology consists of worshipping in the appropriate seasons at the respective shrines of Saints Moritz and Tropez. Mauritius is said to have been despatched by an irritated Roman emperor to lead the Theban auxiliaries against the rebellious Christians in Gaul but, being converted, he revolted along with his troops in the Valais and was, naturally, martyred. But even if this is merely an early travel agent's tale it is true that at least two European towns still bear his name. In the Isère Valley, Bourg St Maurice, which was originally a Roman settlement, is called after him; and, farther east in the Grisons, he was honoured as the patron saint of a church around which grew the town of St Moritz, first recorded in 1139.

One remaining sign of the town's religious connections is the leaning tower which is all that remains of a much earlier church. High above the lake and the village itself, the tower, designed like a cruder version of an Italian campanile, may well have served as a signpost to early travellers and is still useful for orientating oneself in the village. It is odd how leaning towers— this small one, whose incline has developed only gradually with the passage of years, and the more celebrated ones at Pisa and Bologna—have always fascinated those who nourish the unworthy hope that they will be there to see the final collapse.

Winter visitors who return in the summer get a bonus—the surprise of seeing what lay under the snow on their last visit. Much of the village would certainly be disguised by snow during the winter months and, in any event, purposeful skiers on their way to the funicular, or thirsty ones returning to Hanselmann's, would have little time, or inclination, to observe the extravagances of Engadine architecture. But now that it is no longer obligatory to gaze anxiously up at the conditions on the slopes and there is no guilty complex about sauntering idly through the cafés knowing that the more virile are active on the pistes, it is possible to take a fresh look at St Moritz.

The Engadine Valley not only has its own language—in St Moritz itself Ladin, one of the Romansch dialects—it has an indigenous culture which, unobtrusive though it is, has successfully withstood the cosmopolitan influence that waves of tourists from foreign countries have brought with them. The original tradition can still be seen in the individual style of the, invariably, neat and well-maintained houses in the village, or in the farmhouses throughout the valley, or in the Alpine fairs and festivals, or in the elaborate needlework of native dresses.

The domestic style is well shown in the rooms which comprise the Engadine Museum at St Moritz. In this substantial stone building, itself like a typical prosperous Engadine dwelling-house, a number of rooms, taken from houses about to be demolished for one reason or another, have been re-erected to show something of the history of the area. An inspection of the individual rooms is much the easiest way to visualise what life was like in this part of the Grisons during earlier periods: it will also stimulate ideas for contemporary interior decoration. Nearly all the rooms have panelling, or a ceiling, of arolla or cembra pine. This wood is much admired in the Engadine, since the trees seldom grow below 5000 ft. and even in the mountains are becoming scarcer; it has a lingering scent and a pleasant uniform texture. The arches of the doors and the corners of the house are decorated with sgraffito, an Italian process of applying a final coat of white mortar and impressing a pattern on it before it becomes hard.

On the site of the museum, which faces south towards St Moritz-Bad, there is an interesting three-storeyed arcade copied from one which can still be found in Lower Schuls. The ground floor houses a characteristic Engadine parlour, taken from the Albertini house in Zuos, highly redolent of the bourgeois atmosphere of the area. Another room on the first floor, brought from Brail in the Lower Engadine, is more immediately recognisable for its resemblance to the traditional Swiss chalet formed of wooden chips built up to form their own wall. This room bears an inscription dated 1580. On this floor, too, is the show-piece from the same Albertini house, the '*stuva bella*', or best parlour. Next to it is the State chamber which belonged to the Marca family from Mesocco, dated 1621, with some richly carved furniture. The second floor contains a corridor decorated with a remarkable sgraffito frieze copied from a house at Samaden. It shows children riding on grotesque animals, with their procession interrupted at convenient intervals to allow the display of the coat of arms of prominent local families. Two small rooms from Präsanz and Savognino in Oberhalbstein complete this floor. There are many other *objets d'art* of the kind normally found in folk collections, but those in the Engadine Museum seem to retain a lifelike connection with the area. There is, for example, an old hand-pump fire engine from Süs dated 1796 which must have stretched the arms of the local fire brigade much quicker than it put out even the smallest conflagration. Models of chamois and bear traps remind the visitor that it is not long since other forms of prey were hunted by the natives; and, as a final act of historic piety, the remains of a marble statue—said to be the local Roman deity—brought from the summit of the Julier Pass are preserved in the museum.

The native tradition, still alive, can be seen even more clearly in the villages which lie round the edge of the valley or beside the lakes. Their white walls, seen against the Alpine scenery, defy the visitor not to succumb, albeit reluctantly, to the adjective 'picturesque'. They shelter a carefully preserved local culture seldom found elsewhere at heights where the rigours of farming and cattle breeding occupy attention throughout the year. The continuous nature of these settlements contrasts with the forward-looking planning and architecture

belonging to the different periods to be found in the various
tourist centres and in St Moritz. In the villages themselves an
Italian influence has been prevalent since the Duke of Parma
first came over the Bernina Pass. It imparts a grace and lightness
of touch not often found in Alpine heights. Traces of this
abound for those who want to see—the delicate pattern of
the grilles before the deep-sunk windows, the design of the
wrought-iron railings on the balconies, the strangely baroque
nature of the door-knockers and, on the walls, the heraldic
emblazonments which seem to have been perpetually coveted
by the Engadiners. If one had to look for the most typical
Engadine village which still preserved its original simplicity the
authorities would recommend Zuos on the road to the lower
part of the valley. Samaden, which houses the library on which
the study of the Romansch language is based, also retains much
of its original atmosphere.

Italian art can, predictably, be most easily seen in the
churches of the area. Three Romanesque buildings are usually
singled out for particular notice and, while no one would claim
that they have aspired to the excellence of the great Italian
masters themselves, or are as completely satisfying as the famous
Romanesque abbey at Vezelay, they have their own intrinsic
merit. The church of San Gian down the hill at Celerina, and
that of Santa Maria slightly further away at Pontresina, are the
first two. Santa Maria is an impressive vaulted church whose
apse and nave are liberally decorated with episodes in the life of
Christ and the apostles, and the story of Mary Magdalene.
There are Romanesque fragments which recall earlier Byzantine
inspiration and combine with later frescoes from the Quattro-
cento: an elaborate mixture whose total effect is remarkably
pleasant. Further away, in the valley of Fex, the Crasta Chapel
contains reproductions of St Anna, the Virgin Mary, the apostles
and saints who are found elsewhere in local churches.

It is not, however, just to study the excellence of native
culture, or the lively preservation of old traditions, that the
summer visitor comes to St Moritz. There are at least as

interesting examples of surviving local ethos to be found elsewhere; for example, in the Jura, the Tyrol or the Apennines. At St Moritz, however, there is so much else besides. There is perhaps the greatest asset of all, the invisible one, the air. The great medical mystery, why it is so agreeable to breathe in St Moritz, will now be revealed.

As we know, the village lies in an Alpine valley much broader than usually found at its height of 6000 ft. above sea-level. It has a vast, open southern exposure and is surrounded by wooded slopes. The basic point is that at this altitude the air is 18 per cent less dense than it is at sea-level. The temperature, as is to be expected, diminishes with increasing height, but the air itself becomes purer. The sunlight becomes stronger and (as the unwary who overdo incautious sunbathing find to their blistered cost) the ultra-violet rays become more penetrating. Even in the hottest summer, when the days are full of sunshine, the temperature at night can be quite low with even an occasional touch of frost: nothing could be more refreshing after a long day in the sun—in the confident expectation that another similar one will follow. There is, however, a single feature which distinguishes St Moritz's climate from those of other mountain stations: the St Moritz Kurverein point with conviction to the summing up by Professor Jaccoud of Paris in 1873. After studying the level of the barometer, the solar radiation, and the temperature, during the summer months, he concluded that:

> A mean temperature which is higher than would correspond to the height above sea-level, a reduction of the barometric pressure which is, as elsewhere, proportional to the altitude—these are the two contrasting conditions which are not realised together in any other place known to me; and these unique circumstances are in my eyes the basis of the special curative indications of the climate of St Moritz.

To what extent is the worthy visitor aware of this profound

scientific conclusion? The visitor requires oxygen and the oxygen which he will need is more, rather than less, at a height of 6000 ft., as will be apparent from a slight feeling of breathlessness on first arrival. In cruder terms, since the supply of oxygen in the air has been reduced by 18 per cent, and since he must still get the oxygen he requires, the visitor must breathe either more quickly or more deeply. The physician will now observe that, since the body, with little delay, will begin to use as little effort as it can, the result is to deepen the breathing. This is more economical than increasing its speed and, in consequence, the Lowlander's breathing when he arrives at St Moritz will soon become deeper and the single inhalation will become more satisfying. In short, the mountain climate of St Moritz requires deeper breathing which, in turn, contributes to an indefinable, but unmistakable, sense of well-being. Swiss doctors add that the combined effect of the peculiar properties of the Mauritius spring (the mixture of iron and carbonic acid) and the climate is much greater than the single effect of either the spring or the climate.

It would be misleading to suggest an image of visitors to St Moritz involved in perpetual deep-breathing exercises to the sound of rhythmic music or the command of the gymnastic instructor. All that happens is that after a few days' residence the visitor becomes gradually aware that his lungs are functioning with unusual efficiency and he will begin to enjoy all the conventional summer sports which the Kurverein take pains to provide. The altitude has its effect on them too. In the thinner air it is possible to drive a golf ball immense distances, and novice golfers can soon be seen pursuing the mirage of a lower handicap. Tennis, too, has to be played with special balls to compensate for the loss in air density. But there are very few sports to which St Moritz does not make its own contribution. There is a lot of concentration on the various branches of equitation and riders can be found on the bridle-paths, at the jumping paddock or, on occasion, at the indoor riding school. The lakes invite sunbathers and swimmers, and the St Moritz

Lake in particular has favourable air currents for sailing enthusiasts. Ballooning, which made an early appearance in St
Moritz before the first war, is, unfortunately, seldom practised
nowadays, but gliders can still be seen pursuing their disdain-
ful, silent course across the valley, starting either from the air-
field at Samaden or, more sharply, by a catapult fixed from the
top of Muottas Muragl. All these sports and pastimes are practised locally with great enjoyment, but they provoke little in the
way of philosophical reflection. Angling is another matter.

The waters of the River Inn flow in an uninterrupted course
of 200 miles until they reach the Danube, and it is from the
Danube that the Engadine fish start their journey to the lakes
in the valley. They are good, sporting fish and confirm once
more the verity of Ogden Nash's maxim:

> For things are frequently what they seem,
> And this is wisdom's crown
> Only the game fish swims up stream
> The sensible fish swims down.

They arrive in May/June, with a few laggards bringing up the
rear in July. This is summer fishing at its best, and it has been
strangely overlooked by Anglo-Saxon anglers. It is the case that
loch or lake fishing is sometimes despised by the keen fisherman, and lake fishing in Switzerland, in particular, has been
greatly underrated. True, there is perhaps not the same sense of
exalted struggle as there is in river fishing, not the same man-
to-fish combat when the wading angler hooks a ducal salmon,
but it is not everyone who wants to expend all his sportive
energy on a continuous epic struggle, and the Engadine lakes
have much to offer.

The first great attraction of lake fishing is that there is plenty
of space for manœuvre once the fish is hooked: it is a fair fight
with no incidental snags, no branches or huge boulders to
intervene. But it is not all one-sided, and the fish also has
more room to move. A lively trout will lead his adversary a
noble dance. It will rush two or three times, take the line

right out to the backing, and leap in the sunlight at a surprising distance from the boat. There is no more glorious sight than a trout played up and down the golden path made by the sun's reflection on the lake to the sound, as Moray McLaren has described it, of the singing reel. Then, too, all lake fishers are imbued by a sense of the mystery of what lies beneath the glassy surface of the lake. It may be some descendant of an ice-age fish, or a green-backed reptile, and the opaque nature of the water, by itself, keeps the angler's curiosity alive—curiosity whetted every time the hooked, and now tired, fish comes to the side of the boat, takes fright and dives again into the depths.

There are fifteen miles of fishing in the Engadine from Maloja to the point where the glacier waters of the Flaz join the Inn. They stretch from the large lakes in the centre—St Moritz, Silvaplana and Segl—to smaller ones at a distance. The natives find Lake Sgrischus, 6000 ft. up in the Fex Valley, one of the most attractive, and the 'evening rise' can reach remarkable proportions with an effect enhanced by the scenery. Others which are particularly commended are Lake Grevasalvas, a small lake on the Julier Pass, and the Suvretta Lake to the north of Piz Julier. But there are many others, and one of the main attractions of fishing in the Engadine in the summer is the sudden realisation that small lakes, which had been either invisible or unnoticed in the winter season, now lie patent to the gaze and full of fish. All the way from the Hahnensee, below Corvatsch, to Lake Muragl and right down to the Lago Nero and Lago Della Crocetta on the Bernina Pass, the lakes can provide surprisingly rich catches.

The lakes are well stocked and the Engadine fisher can look for the usual lake and river varieties of trout, together with rainbow, golden rainbow and that most ancient fish the char. Most anglers have a special affection for the char. It has a beautiful appearance, its flesh is firm and pink and it is delicious to eat. It is one of the oldest of all fish, dating from the ice age, and lies deep in the lake. Engadine fishing is also unique in allowing

A familiar figure:
Bobby Locke in play

Summer ski-ing on Corvatsch

A typical Engadine house: Schloss von Salis in Soglio

The high life in the twenties

. . . . and in the fifties

A famous name on the
Cresta: Winston
Churchill, Jnr, with
Serge Ovsiesky, 1952

Hold tight: Elsa Maxwell
and Gunther Sachs, 1955

The Duke and Duchess
of Kent, 1964

Princess Marina
at the Army Ski
Championships, 1960

Alfred Hitchcock:
Hullo, hullo, hullo

It was all a mistake,
officer

Sir Francis Chichester
with two familiar
St Moritz figures—
Mr Albert Candrian and
Josef Netzer

The Shah of Persia and
family at Piz Nair, 1967

St Sylvester: Christian Onassis with the traditional pig:
1st January 1971

the angler to use almost any known method—the fly, the
spinner or live bait. This in itself is proof of the richness of the
fishing grounds which can withstand depredations by those who
stoop to the mechanical device of the spinner, as well as expert
anglers with the fly who boast that 'they troll not, neither do
they spin'. In the Silvaplana Lake a trout weighing 40 lb. has
been hooked, and in the Sils Lake one, which must have been a
cannibal, measuring 3 ft. 6 in. in length has been landed. 8⅔ in.
is the smallest fish that can be retained; anything smaller goes
back into the water to grow. The variety in the Engadine lakes
is such that here, more than many places, the angler can indulge
in his final reverie at the prospect of the giant fish which is still
waiting for him. He may, in the winter, have already done his
longest ski-ing trip, or his fastest run on the slalom course, or
his best time on the Cresta; he may know that age is atrophying
his muscles and that he will not improve on these times; but
still he has every reason to think that the really large fish for
which he has searched all his life is still lying beneath the surface
of the Silvaplana Lake and may soon come to the fly. The most
rewarding baskets are caught in showers of rain, and by any
European standards the fishing is remarkably cheap.

Anglers are a race apart. They prefer to practise their
mysteries in decent privacy and are seldom enthusiastic at the
appearance of spectators, either on the bank or aboard competing craft on the surface of the lake. Only in solitude can the
personal relationship between the fisherman and the fish be
properly manifested. The smaller Alpine lakes will, as a rule,
afford fishing without interruption: but on the larger lakes
there are yachtsmen or swimmers, although this does not
appear to have a notably adverse effect on the size of the basket.
And there are compensating advantages for the St Moritz
fisher. While most anglers have to be prepared to endure
conditions of extreme discomfort—both as regards weather and
the Spartan nature of their hostelry when the day's fishing is
over—the Engadine has an equable climate and no one can say
that the hotels lack comfort. Even in St Moritz, however, as the

I

happy angler dozes off in the hotel lounge after dinner, his hand and arm will still twitch occasionally in an alarming manner: but there is no cause for anxiety: it is not the beginning of *rigor mortis*. The explanation is simple. Just as the semi-dormant bob driver in winter can still feel the abrasive effect of the ropes against his hand, so the sleepy angler can feel the gentler tug as the trout takes the bait, and automatically makes to tighten his line in reply.

For those who are not attracted by musing on the surface of the lakes and who are unimpressed by the great volume of persuasive literature on angling from Izaac Walton onwards, there are other ways in which the visitor can identify himself with the landscape at St Moritz. The valley of the Engadine has probably more pathways laid out than any other comparable area, and the St Moritz Kurverein alone is responsible for maintaining some seventy-five miles of byways. For the most part, these paths follow the natural contours without artificial construction. There is, however, something of a dilemma here. The paths are clearly marked so that the walker will not lose his way and will know where he is going, but this in itself intrudes on the natural partnership between the walker and the countryside by imposing a slightly artificial element. The sense of exploration is missing. The pleasure in the pathless woods, the rapture on the lonely shore, have both been lost. With this minor reservation it must be admitted that nowhere is walking more stimulating whether along the pleasant shores of the lakes or much higher up in the real mountain area.

Two examples will suffice to illustrate the variety. At the lower level a footpath along the left shores of the lakes from Maloja goes past the cembra pines near Isola to the Fex Brook in the direction of Sils. The Fex Valley which, like the lake of Sils itself, is a nature reserve, is bound to be one of the rambler's objectives. There is no competition from motor-cars and from June onwards the territory from Platta to the edge of the Fex glacier is completely covered with a carpet of flowers in full bloom. From the lake of Silvaplana the visitor will be keen to turn off to Alp and Fuorcla Surlej—if he thinks that his lungs will stand it—and make for the very rewarding high-altitude walk which affords one of the best views of the Bernina group. The great ice pyramid of Piz Roseg, flanked by Piz Scerscen, with Piz Morteratsch and the Jacob's ladder of the Bernina-Bianco ridge, are all clearly visible. The descent from the Fuorcla can be made either along the slope above the Hahnensee towards St Moritz or down into the Val Roseg. Those who have skied in the Corvatsch area in the winter will be intrigued to detect what were the snow-covered pistes among the mountain paths.

The more energetic, by whom we mean the amateur mountaineers in the strict sense of the word, will be tempted to start from Pontresina and tackle perhaps the dome-like Piz Palu or Bella Vista by way of Diavolezza. If their technique and nerve are adequate, they can then make the classic tour of the Bernina, the highest peak in the Grisons (13,285 ft.), first climbed in 1850, after spending the night in the Boval hut (8058 ft.). There is also the temptation to try Piz Morteratsch itself (12,317 ft.) or try to see the ibexes on Piz Albris (10,400 ft.).

It is not, however, only the indolent ambler or the well-thewed mountaineer who can enjoy the summer climate at St Moritz, since the Engadine Valley is pre-eminently the place where the botanist, or the simple flower-lover, really comes into his own. The climate is particularly favourable to him—a climate where larches and cembra pines can be seen on northern slopes up to 8500 ft., more than 2000 ft. higher than in the Tyrol, and where the permanent snow-line lies at 10,100 ft., compared with 7500 ft. in the Bavarian Alps, and 9000 ft. in the Pyrenees. In the valleys of the Engadine there flourishes a rich plant life which has no rival elsewhere in the Alps. In addition to native flowers there are those which have come from the eastern and western Alps or from the lower Poschiavo Valley. From surprisingly early in the year the St Moritz meadows grow centaury, silver thistles and rampion. Alpine asters, mountain arnica and the snow gentian, which are normally discovered at much greater heights, are also found in the Engadine at the lakeside.

The beginning of spring in the Engadine is celebrated by the schoolchildren singing their traditional Romansch song:

> *Chalanda Marz, Chaland' Avrigl,*
> *laschè las vachas our d'uvigl,*
> *Cha l'èrva crescha e la naiv svanescha!*
> (First of March, first of April,
> let the cow out of the byre,
> so that the grass will grow and
> the snow will go!)

As the snows melt, the coming of spring is also marked by the appearance of the soldanella, and by the middle of April the Engadine spring flowers are in their full bloom—when elsewhere in the central Alps the snow still covers the ground. By now, those most delicate flowers, the mountain and spring anemones, can be seen, with the stalkless and the small blue spring gentian and, soon after the heather, the Alpine crowfoot.

More surprising is the abundant growth of Alpine species at much higher altitudes, even over 8000 ft. Rare arctic flowers which have survived from the ice age still obstinately flourish here, and the edelweiss grows up to 10,000 ft., together with the most ambitious of all Alpine flowers, the pale pink glacier crowfoot. The flowers which grow in the Engadine Valley are of such a quality and grow in such quantity that to complete the picture it seems right to name the most striking representatives of the Engadine flora and give some suggestions about where they may be found. There is no guarantee that all these species can be immediately found, but the chances, even for the layman, are fairly high, and the most remarkable feature is perhaps the wide prevalence of so many different flowers. The list which follows first appeared in the *Engadine Year Book* before the First World War, but it has since been brought up to date and is still valid.

FLORA OF THE ENGADINE

Senecio carniolicus. A species of Groundsel. Covered with fine grey hairs. Flowers orange yellow. *Languard. Bernina. Val Bevers. Camegaskertal.* July–August.

Etrichium nanum. Dwarf Scorpion Grass. A pretty, silky plant, growing on Alpine pastures. Corolla of a pure brilliant blue, with yellow throat. *Languard. Ot. Crasta Mora on the Albula. Bernina. Heutal. Corvatsch.* July–August.

Gentiana purpurea. Purple Gentian. Corolla bell-shaped. Rose-like fragrance. *Common on pastures.* July–August.

Pedicularis tuberosa. Tuberous Louse Wort. Corolla yellow, upper lip long. *On almost all pastures.* July–August.

Soldanella pusilla. Delicate Soldanella. A pretty little bell-shaped flower, the first herald of the Alpine spring. A frail little plant blossoming close to the melting snow. Flowers one or two on a stem, funnel-shaped; copper-red, passing into a bluish tint. *On all Alpine pastures and in snowy hollows.* July–August.

Gentiana tenella. Tender Gentian. Blossoms solitary, long-stalked. Corolla violet to white, four-lobed. Rare. Meadows, sand, snowy hollows. *Albula Pass. Morteratsch. Val Roseg.* July–August.

Linnaea borealis. Boreal Linnaea. (Order Caprifoliaceae.) A very slender evergreen shrub, creeping on the mossy carpet of the Alpine forests, especially in the zone of the larches and cembra pines, but not ascending to the Alpine region proper. Leaves oval, opposite; flower stem forked, each branch bearing a bell-shaped blossom of a faint red or white colour, with blood-red stripes inside. *Near the Kurhaus St Moritz. Süs. Tarasp. Pontresina.* July–September.

Primula longiflora. Long-tubed Primula. Fresh-coloured flowers forming an umbel, at the end of a long stalk. *Sils-Maria. Valley of Fex. Alp Grüm.* June–July.

Hutchinsia brevicaulis. Short-stemmed Alpine Cress. (Order Cruciferae.) Pretty white blossoms. *Bernina. Ot. Padella. Minschun. Curver. Lavirun.* June–August.

Gentiana nivalis. Snow Gentian. A rarity among Alpine plants. Stem upright, slender, simple, or branched above. Flowers solitary or few, short-stalked. The tiny bright blue blossoms of this species of gentian are among the most charming flowers to be found in the Alps. *Near Sils and Pontresina, in the plains.* July–September.

Sempervivum arachnoideum. Cobwebbed Houseleek. This species of Houseleek is easily recognised by its globose rosettes of very fleshy leaves covered with loose, cobweb-like hairs, and its panicled cymes of red-purple flowers. Dry places, sunny rocks. *Common throughout the Upper Engadine.* July–August.

Pyrola minor. Lesser Winter-green. Stem ascending. Flowers small, white, often tinged with pale red. *Pontresina. St Moritz.* July.

Saxifraga biflora. Two-blossomed Saxifrage. Stem perennial, creeping, much branched. Flowers two or three at the end of short stalks, white or rose-red. Near the snow-line. *Throughout the Upper Engadine.* June–August.

Aconitum napellus. Blue Monkshood. Stem strong, erect. Lower leaves petioled, upper sessile, dark green, divided. Flowers on upright stems forming a conspicuous panicle. Sepals large, dark blue, the dorsal one hooded, hence the English name. A poisonous weed. *On all high pastures.* June–August.

Gnaphalium supinum. Dwarf Cudweed. A small tufted plant. Bracts brown. Flowers yellowish white. Often forms a dense turf in the hollows, and is eagerly devoured by the sheep. *Val Roseg. Bernina.* June–August.

Ranunculus glacialis. Glacier Crowfoot. Calyx thickly covered with reddish brown or blackish hairs; corolla white to red outside, persistent after blossoming. (This characteristic differentiates *R. glacialis* from all other species of Crowfoot.) By the side of glaciers, on granite. On the highest peaks and ridges; ascends higher than any other of the Swiss flowering plants. *Bernina. Scaletta.* June–September.

Ranunculus parnassifolius. Parnassia-leaved Crowfoot. Sessila leaves, roundish heart-shaped, with strong ribs, hairy on the upper surface, bluish green; calyx and flower stalks woolly. *Albula. Piz Ot. Bevers pastures.* July–August.

Saxifraga bryoides. Moss-like Saxifrage. Forms moss-like, close-growing rosettes. Flowers white. In the rocky crevices of the summits and high peaks. *Roseg. Bernina. Val Bevers. Albula.* July–September.

Leontopodium alpinum (*Gnaphalium Leontopodium*). The Edelweiss. Easily recognised by its woolly covering. Leaves linear-

lanceolate, very woolly, especially underneath. Several blossoms
unite at the end of the stalk to form a dense umbel, which is surrounded by several white, woolly leaves disposed in the form of a
star, like the petals of a composite flower. On rocky slopes and bells
of turf. *Throughout the Upper Engadine.* July–September.

Campanula cenisia. Mount Cenis Bellflower. Distinguishable
by its recumbent stem bearing only one, rarely two to three flowers,
and by its deeply lobed corolla. Flowers erect, light blue. *Pischa.*
Piz Vadret. Albula. Piz Mezzem. August.

Rhododendron ferrugineum. Rust-red Alpenrose. A small
shrub, recumbent or erect. Leaves lanceolate, leathery, smooth
revolute, rust-red, and hairy on the under side. Blossoms in cymes,
corolla funnel-shaped, light red to dark purple, rarely white,
glandular spots on the flowers and flower-stalks. *Throughout the
Upper Engadine.* July–September.

Artemisia mutellina. Wormwood. A composite flower, recognisable by the strong odour of its silky, finely divided leaves. Flowers
light yellow. On sunny rocks of the highest Alps. *Bernina. Roseg.*
Val Fex. Saluver. Albula. June–July.

Trifolium alpinum. Alpine clover. The most beautiful and the
sweetest scented of our clovers. Easily recognised by its narrow
leaflets, its large sessile heads with few flowers, its delicious fragrance, and its large tough rootstock. *Throughout the Upper Engadine.*
June–September.

Achillea moschata. Musk Milfoil. (Iva.) Stem erect, spreading,
ray-flowers white. Leaves strongly aromatic, especially when rubbed.
Alpine pastures. Primitive rocks. *Bernina. Roseg.* June–July.

Nigritella angustifolia. Scented Nigritella. An orchis remarkable for its strong vanilla-like odour. The lip of the flower and the
short spur are turned upwards—in most of the other species of
orchis they turn downwards. Flowers brownish red. On high pastures
and in meadows. *On all the high pastures of the Upper Engadine.*
July–August.

Lychnis alpina. Red Alpine Flycatcher. Belongs to the pink
family (Caryophyllaceae), but has five styles, the real pinks having
only two, the Silene three. *On high pastures, especially on the Albula.*
This variety of Alpine flora has been exhibited at the St Moritz and
Pontresina Flower Shows for several seasons with conspicuous
success.

Aquilegia alpina. Alpine Columbine. Calyx and corolla blue. Petals form prettily curved honeyspurs. It is forbidden to pluck it by Cantonal law.

The combination of green meadows covered with flowers, snow and naked ice—from the beds of the valleys to the peaks of the ridges—forms a contrast which will perpetually stir the imagination. In the words of the Zürich naturalist, Conrad Gressner, in the sixteenth century:

> Such great variety as in the mountains, and within confines so narrow, is to be found in no place else. For to say nothing more, there we can see and live through the four seasons, summer, autumn, winter and spring, all in a single day.

9

The High Life

There is an interesting enigma about the high life at St Moritz which has painfully perplexed those who have written about it, whether they are gossip journalists or more profound social historians. The high life is both a hoax and a reality.

It is, subjectively, a hoax in the sense that it is not necessary to be entered in the *Almanach de Gotha*, or *Debrett* or, simply, to be very rich to enjoy a season at St Moritz. Not only topical tycoons, like Sir Charles Clore, or regal descendants of ancient lineage, like the Shah of Persia, find pleasure in the Grisons. Incidentally, the Shah's purchase of the Villa Suvretta reveals an unusual aberration in taste. Perhaps the least distinguished architecturally of all the houses in St Moritz, it is self-consciously at odds with its surroundings and is immediately recognisable as an excellent study in Victorian suburbia. The gloomy exterior has been only marginally improved by the addition of a large canopy in beaten brass bearing the imperial insignia to shelter the present occupant of the Peacock Throne when he arrives in his Lamborghini. But those who inhabit humbler quarters—through package tours, in pensions or the smaller hotels—find that all the various delights of St Moritz are equally available to them. The illusion of the high life is equally theirs, and only the sternest ascetics would deny a sense of vicarious satisfaction when a little (frozen) blue blood appeared to drop on them, too, from time to time.

The reality is that the high life proper, nostalgically like a monument to what now seems almost a prehistoric age, also survives. The most dramatic example is the Corviglia Club. Between the wars it occurred to some senior *habitués* of the Palace Hotel and other luxurious establishments that their favourite hostelries were becoming too congested, and they decided to migrate up the hillside to Corviglia for their private entertainment. The Corviglia Club was accordingly formed in 1930 under the Presidency of the Duc de Sangro, supported by a committee which included such egregious sportsmen as Compte Theo Rossi di Montelera, Marquis de La Falaise, Duc d'Albe, Harry Hays Morgan, Prince Constantin de Lichtenstein, Stanley Mortimer, Stavros Niarchos and George H. Page.

The club premises, favoured by the gods, have an enviable prospect across the valley. They are owned by the members and, as in all really exclusive clubs, the subscription is small, amounting to 1000 Swiss francs for life. The social tone of the membership, which varies between 100 and 150, is rigorously maintained under the zealous care of the committee whose principal officers are now the Prince of Liechtenstein and Baron Erwein Gecmen-Waldek. Banquets are prepared and served by the staff from the Chesa Veglia in the village and the only mysteries practised within the confines which have filtered through to the public are the moonlight parties at the height of the season. The Kurverein reports with impressive objectivity that the Corviglia members have their own club ties, emblems and buttons.

Situated at the busiest point of ski-ing activity, the Corviglia Club—and this is the real point of the story—attracts little envy. Even those who have no prospect of passing through its sacred portals will point to it with pride. It recalls a prodigal, privileged past and social glories that have, for the most part, vanished. This harmless remembrance of things past resembles the more satirical evocation in Sandy Wilson's *Valmouth*. In his adaptation of Firbank—surely the one musical which should always be revived—he recalls, through the eyes of three long-ago debs, a time when:

The sun was always shining
In a bright blue sky above.
And we were always frantically,
Romantically,
In love.

That other time, that other place,
Is where we all belong;
Where all the gals were pretty
And all the men were strong.

Do you remember Coco Fooks,
Flossie St Vincent and Bimbo Stooks:
Twirby Rogers and Bushy Ames:
They all of them had such expressive names.

And the Duke of Crewe on a great black nag
In hunting pink with the Valmouth Drag;
And Monkey Trotter in Guardsman's rig
Doing a rather suggestive jig.

And Princess Soboya who came to stay
And changed her tiara twice a day.
And Lorna Van Hoff with her turquoise hair
Who once ran nude through the market square.

And Bungay Sussex—the Earl, I mean,
Who used old brandy as brilliantine;
And Violet Blogg who eloped with a sheikh
And was always drunk during Holy Week.

How fine they were: how sublime they were:
How great and grand in their prime they were.
They were bold and beautiful,
Brave and true;

And it goes without saying
That we were too.

An extravagant quotation, offered without apology, which suggests its moral in the last line. And who is to say that this harmless *snobbisme*—indulged in at St Moritz by visitors who stay for only ten days or a fortnight—is not to be preferred to a society which is elsewhere 'one polish'd horde, formed of two mighty tribes, the bores and bored'? Is there not something to be said in favour of applying instead Sydney Smith's aphorism and saying of St Moritz: 'Ah, you flavour everything; you are the vanilla of society'?

From the time when the Grand Tour, undertaken by the nobility and their imitators, gave way to tourism, described in more detail in our earlier chapters and possibly dating from Thomas Cook's first 'personally conducted tour' of Switzerland in 1864, St Moritz has always been associated with some form of high life, and with a feeling of being lifted out of one's normal existence. It seems very probable that the sense of achievement in actually arriving contributes something to this euphoria. In the same way that the small Republic of San Marino, perched high above the Emilian Plain, owes its precarious individual existence to its remoteness and height, St Moritz, protected on all sides by serrated mountain ridges, seems to be the capital of a small kingdom of its own. And the satisfaction of accomplishing something by getting there is enhanced if the visitor has arrived in a suitably receptive frame of mind—in our view, by train.

It is possible to reach St Moritz by travelling by plane to Samaden, or by car over one of the five passes, but the sybaritic way is still in a railway carriage. Rail travel throughout Europe has lost much of its glamour; it is no longer the main ambition of the experienced traveller to board the Orient Express at Ostend and eat, drink or sleep in luxury on at least part of the way to Vienna, Budapest and Istanbul. Saturnine, whiskered attendants in blue and gold uniform do not now usher you to the comfort of a lace-pillowed seat in an atmosphere of hock and seltzer and Turkish cigarettes by Sullivan Powell.

Before the first war the traveller was most likely to come from London on the Engadine Express 'composed of sleeping, restaurant and baggage cars only'. He would leave Victoria at the comfortable hour of eleven o'clock in the morning and, travelling by Calais and then by sleeper to Zürich, he would reach St Moritz just after midday on the following day, for the first-class single fare of £6 13s. 2d. Today he is more likely to fly to Zürich and take the train to Chur before embarking on the Rhätische Bahn for the last two hours of his journey. The Rhätische Bahn, although it now shows distressing signs of modernity, still maintains a few antique coaches and two engines to push them up the steep gradients. For long owned by a private company, the décor of the compartments is still as it was fifty years ago. The dining-room is heavily panelled, green baize prevents contact with the frozen windows, and there is a lot of polished brass everywhere. The stewards, with their striped aprons, complete the Victorian illusion. As the train pants slowly round the hairpin bends to reach Samaden and Celerina, the snow-capped villages sink into the depths of the valleys. Growing pressure on the eardrums is a warning that 5000 ft. has been reached, and the freezing dry air on emergence at St Moritz leaves the traveller in no doubt that he is well and truly in the Alps. It is, however, better organised now than it was in Thomas Cook's early days. He used to complain that when one of his parties arrived there was an unseemly scrimmage and he had:

> to contend against the eagerness of young and active gentlemen who would run off from the stations to secure the best rooms and to bespeak them for others of their immediate association. I checked this impetuosity by requesting hotel-keepers to send first-comers, as the most vigorous, to the highest rooms.

A determinedly extrovert existence: that, at first glance, is the image which life at St Moritz presents to the outside world. It is the same, or very nearly the same, at all places which are visited primarily for pleasure and enjoyment. But no one should believe that unrelieved heartiness prevails round the clock. There is something at St Moritz, maybe the feeling of the high mountains that haunted Byron, which induces odd moments of retrospection. Many visitors to Venice have noted that, amid the revelry in that most civilised, urbane and amusing of cities, the gondolas look sad and add a touch of bitter-sweet to the confection. It is so at St Moritz, and no one can for long remain immune to the splendour of the landscape.

The great painter of the Alps, and of the Engadine in particular, was Giovanni Segantini, and it is only fitting that the main collection of his works should have been assembled in the elegant small museum at St Moritz which bears his name. Segantini is of much interest, not only for his artistic achievements but also for himself. More than any other painter, he has succeeded in capturing the basic elements of Alpine scenery: the space, the perspective, the enormous distances and the changing light and shade of clouds on the snow. He was a man of aggressive integrity and, although only his last years were free from privation, he remained throughout obsessed by the concept of man's place in nature, and his last words are said to have been: 'Let me look out on my mountains.'

Segantini was born in 1858 at Arco in the Trentino, but his mother died when he was five and his father took him to Milan to live with his half-sister. Life was not easy for him there and there was a spell in a reformatory school. After surviving smallpox he worked for a while as an apprentice in his stepbrother's pharmacy at Borgo in Val Sugana. It was only when his stepbrother recognised his unusual ability and sent him to Milan to study art that his career really started. Later his luck turned and he established a long-term and friendly business relationship with two brothers who owned an art gallery and who were willing to take his work. This allowed him to settle at Pusiano on Lake Brianza where he stayed for four years and produced many enchanting paintings of the joys and sorrows of country life. But he was always attracted by the spectacle of the mountains and in 1886 he went to live at Savognino in Oberhalbstein beyond the Julier Pass. There he stayed for eight years until he moved to his final home at Maloja in 1894. During his last five years his fame spread beyond the frontiers of Switzerland and he was recognised at international exhibitions in Amsterdam, Paris and Turin.

The most compelling features of Segantini's work are his unusual technique and his comprehension of space. While he was experimenting with light and colour at Savognino, he devised a new method of applying colours as pure as possible, instead of blending them beforehand on his palette. When the finished work is seen from a distance the colours appear to blend of their own accord and the vibrations perceived by the eye give them additional light. This technique, in which Segantini was undoubtedly the pioneer, came to be known as '*divisionismo*'. In retrospect, it looks as though he was trying to achieve the same result as the Pointillistes, but by a slightly different method. Many of his drawings show something of the same apocalyptic vision as William Blake, and his peasant scenes have been compared to those of Millet or Courbet. But it is for his larger works that he is best remembered. Principal of these was the great triptych *Birth–Life–Death*, which remained unfinished. The first section, depicting peasant life in the high mountains, shows the Alpine sun illuminating a distant massif. The second painting shows an evening vision of the mountains round the Engadine Valley when the sun has set; the rays still light the sky and flocks are being led homewards. The third, and final, section shows a freezing winter scene at Maloja with the first rays of the morning sun beginning to touch the mountains. Taken together, these three paintings realise Segantini's wish to set out man's place against the glory of the natural landscape. Segantini does not now command a widely known reputation, except among Alpine enthusiasts, but it is difficult to come away from a visit to his collection without feeling that human experience has been enriched and that he has been seriously underrated as a painter.

The Corviglia Club has been chosen as the most obvious stronghold of the high life, but there are many other outposts where it is equally practised, although perhaps not with such extremes of refinement. Luncheon in the sun, absorbing the ultraviolet rays, is not peculiar to Corviglia. The Zuber Hut, the Alpine restaurant at the top of the first Suvretta ski-tow, and the one owned by the Schweizerhof, are all well-established centres for refreshment out of doors. The Zuber is the largest, with an open patio that can absorb seemingly endless crowds of skiers, all jostling for service at the same time. Here a dilemma appears: is it to be a quick light meal with a glass of grog, then back to the serious business of ski-ing; or the beguiling attraction of a more leisurely lunch with some coffee and kirsch followed by nodding slumber in the sun? The prudent, or the less determinedly athletic, will settle for a strenuous morning, a long lunch and only an odd run in the afternoon. The Suvretta and Schweizerhof restaurants offer variations on the same theme.

By four o'clock, with the sun dipping, at least in the early spring months, the Corviglia cable-car is packed with returning skiers; the bus brings them back from Suvretta; and café society reawakens. Apart from the hotels, there are three great centres for this time of the day: Hanselmann's, Hauser's and the Chesa Veglia. At Hanselmann's, to be contentious, the gâteaux and pastries are probably the best; certainly they could be no better. Hanselmann's also retains an atmosphere of furs and feather boas—the contrast between the latest ski-pants and traditional haute couture is one of the perpetual pleasures at St Moritz—and one always suspects that refugees from Imperial Russia still linger here. Hauser's is more modern and, on occasion, its clients spread over the open terrace in front of it. Hauser's rightly boasts of its whipped marron, and this, above all, is the place for the most delicious hot chocolate. It is always crowded, but eventually there is room for everyone. One couple, their faces deeply tanned from their hours on the slopes, were looking thirstily for a table when a genial, elderly figure rose from his seat and said: 'I would not have you strain your calf muscles further. If I leave you some Swiss francs, will you pay my bill and take my table?' 'Thank you; as always, no one could be more gracious.' They had recognised their benefactor as that greatest of English rugby forwards and former Member of Parliament, Lord Wakefield.

Within the labyrinthine interior of the Chesa Veglia, which boasts a native Engadine décor, lies a café for the afternoons, bars and restaurants. The café is the favourite place for tea dances from four till six o'clock and the unpolished floor resounds to the thump of ski boots in approximate time to the music of an odd Romansch trio. It is never quite clear wherein is found the particular virtue in dancing wearing thick sweaters, ski pants and boots, but this is an art form greatly cherished by devotees, particularly at the Chesa Veglia. A special table is reserved for bobbers (and their admirers) who carry their fame with careless ease, although, from their preoccupied look, some at least are still vibrating at the recollection of navigating the Sunny or Horseshoe bends. Less eminent customers peer from the medieval gallery which looks down on the dance floor, and all is merry as an Engadine bell. Those who prefer some less strenuous diversion may try their luck on the wheel of chance with a game of boule at the Kursaal. The stakes are modest and the play is not wildly exciting. Lacking the panache of the great gambling casinos, boule is appreciated only by addicts.

After the attractions of the *thé dansant* have been exhausted, the Beautiful People mysteriously disappear: some to visit the coiffeur; some for a sauna bath or a swim in one of the grand new swimming pools in the hotels; and some simply to rest.

Then the long day does not close; it comes to life again as the lights begin to twinkle from the rocks and there is a sortie to the bars for the first of the evening's sharpeners. It may be to the American Bar at the Kulm, the Scotch Bar at the Schweizerhof, the Grand Bars at the Palace or Suvretta House, or the exotic one at the Monopol. What makes any bar popular? It must be small enough to enable you to rub shoulders with fellow customers—solitary drinking is a melancholy business—and the

K

design must be very individual. The atmosphere and the service must persuade you that, although you know it is not really true, there is something special about the drinks served. To make a choice among the St Moritz bars would be invidious, but, even at peril, it can be asserted that nowhere is the spirit of St Moritz so well seen as in the Cresta Bar at Steffani's Hotel. Traditionally decorated with wooden panelling, photographs and relics of early Cresta run equipment, it is extraordinarily hospitable, and the champagne cocktails have an extra sparkle.

Now to dinner. It is no part of this book to serve as a good food guide or to attempt a catalogue of Engadine cuisine. Let it suffice that there are enough native dishes available to satisfy the most exacting gourmet who can be found making his nocturnal pilgrimage to the Bernasconi or, perhaps, even farther afield to Talvo on the way to Champfer for a sizzling fondue, or to the Calonder or the Caspar Badrutt where the meals are monotonously famous. In the Schweizerhof the boards are so laden at the Sunday gala dinners that television cameras have been seen focussing on the food instead of the guests. If anyone remains whose appetite is still unsatisfied, it is very likely that he will attempt the longer journey to the Sarazena at Pontresina for its carefully preserved rustic atmosphere.

In the de-luxe establishments the chefs contrive to offer what can best be described as international meals. Rich and succulent though they are, these are strangely similar, and no one blindfold could tell whether he was eating at Suvretta House, the Savoy in London or the Royal Danielli at Venice. Lest this should seem too critical an assessment, however, the altitude at St Moritz plays strange tricks on the palate and diversifies even the most recognisable international dish. This applies, too, to wine, and the native Swiss vintages, particularly those of Dole and Eigel, at least hold their own with more celebrated clarets, hocks and burgundies. The tipster's choice would be the Grill Room at the Kulm, both for the cellar and the cuisine, or the Grill Room at the Chesa Veglia for a dish so full of calories that it could only be consumed by an active skier—baked potato Chesa Veglia, a vast potato in its jacket, stuffed with sour cream and caviare.

Even now the minstrels are tuning up for the evening revelry. If it is a big night there will be the Cresta Ball at the Palace Hotel, a candlelight evening at the Corviglia Club, or one of the numerous galas and cabarets at Suvretta House. Even on what would be elsewhere a very ordinary evening there will still be enough esoteric entertainment in the King's Club at the Palace, hidden in the bowels of the hotel, or in the Sunny Bar at the Kulm where Lord Brabazon of Tara and Gunther Sachs lead the bobbers and Cresta riders in their strange tribal ceremonies. It will by now be apparent that the high life extends far beyond these plutocratic *boîtes de nuit*. The same exhausting joviality can be found elsewhere in the village until the last reluctant reveller stumbles through the snow to snatch a few hours' sleep before taking off once more for the slopes, to return with evangelical fervour to a different (but similar) locale on the next evening. The Hôtel La Margna has a more traditional Grisons atmosphere; and, lastly, the most strenuous dancing to the very end is to be found to the rhythmic beat of the trio in the underground taverna at the Hôtel Caspar Badrutt. To wake the next morning, after spending longer than one meant to in one or many more of these establishments, with a clear eye and no danger of hearing the anvil chorus sounding in one's skull, proves once again the preservative qualities of alcohol taken in the right quantity and the revifying effect of the altitude.

Café complêt and the breathless business of fastening ski boots starts the cycle revolving again without any sign of nausea or disaffection on the part of those who enjoy Alpine holidays. Rich and poor alike are smitten with the fever, and their business and religion is to play. Snow, it seems, provides the broad base of the pyramid, and somewhere between the base and the peak everyone who shares an enthusiasm for snow will find an acceptable, but probably anonymous, place. It is not quite the same in summer, but even then the variety of pursuits which can be practised in the Engadine Valley still has the same effect of conveying a universal, honorary citizenship of a domain whose capital is St Moritz.

The genial catholicity which all pilgrims to St Moritz observe as the town's most characteristic feature derives from the unusual contrasts which are soon apparent. At the one end of the spectrum there is the undisguised opulence of Suvretta House, the Palace, the Kulm and the Carlton; at the other end there are more modest establishments like the Hotel Bären or the Bernasconi, or the various Hôtels Garni (a mysterious expression that means bed and breakfast only). In between there are excellent hostelries like the Chantarella, the Albana and the Posthotel. All have their individual features; all contribute equally to enjoyment. If the most affluent audience is to be found oscillating at the Palace's King's Club discotheque, no less vigour is to be discerned among the nocturnal athletes in the grotto below Steffani's. Both may be visited in a night. And the Chesa Veglia caters for all tastes, purses and inclinations, even including an unusually refined bowling alley.

There is the contrast, too, between the various architectural styles and periods. St Moritz has developed so far from its origins as an Alpine village that few of the earliest buildings have survived. Traces of *la belle epoque* can be found, however, in the main lounge of the Schweizerhof (long patronised by Field Marshal Viscount Montgomery, always greeted by aggressively punctilious salutes from ex-servicemen), and in the low-ceilinged restaurant at Steffani's across the square. But it is one of St Moritz's peculiar achievements to absorb new buildings which offer a contrast but not a conflict. One hotel not so far mentioned—the Hotel Crystal built in the last decade—is a skilful example of urban planning. It has been insinuated into the very heart of the shopping area without any apparent dislocation of the surrounding buildings and, although its modern exterior makes no concession to traditional taste, it does not seem in any way out of place. If it is the forerunner of other new hotels in St Moritz, the conservationists need not fear that any vandals are likely to have their way. This is evident, too, in the new flats and chalets which have appeared since the last war. There are not many towns which could claim with such certainty that they had succeeded in building in the modern idiom with so little adverse effect on the surroundings.

Tourism has been defined as the business of fleecing the tourist, and it has been said as a corollary that the quicker it is done the less painful it will be. The St Moritz hoteliers would scarcely allege that they were in the business for the good of their health, but the number of visitors who return year after year, so that they can almost claim to be St Moritzers, suggests that they have not been subjected to, or at least are not aware of, any violent extraction of Swiss francs from their pockets. In the final appreciation, St Moritz is a place for romantics—for emotion recollected in tranquillity—and the sun is rightly its symbol. But the words of Mercury are harsh after the songs of Apollo and so our story is ended. As in *Love's Labours Lost*: 'You that way: we this way.'

APPENDIX I

Summary of Accommodation in St Moritz

ST MORITZ DORF

		Beds	Front end paper map
Group I	Carlton	200	10
	Kulm	300	15
	Palace	320	24
	Suvretta House	380	
Group II	Caspar Badrutt	100	11
	Chantarella	160	12
	Crystal	160	13
	Monopol	120	22
	Schweizerhof	160	27
Group III	Albana	120	1
	Bellevue	80	6
	Calonder garni	75	9
	La Margna	100	19
	Neues Posthotel	120	23
	Salastrains	40	26
	Steffani	100	29
	Waldhaus	60	32
Group IV	Aurora garni	25	3
	Bären	90	4
	Bellaval (Alkoholfrei)	43	5
	Bernasconi	60	8
	Meierei garni	20	
	Villa Grünenberg garni	30	18

ST MORITZ DORF (*continued*)

		Beds	Front end paper map
Hotels Garni			
Bed and			
Breakfast only	Belvedere	102	7
	Eden	50	14
	Hauser	70	17
	Languard	36	20
	Rosatsch	40	25

ST MORITZ BAD

Group II	Du Lac	200	37
	Kurhaus	250	39
Group III	Chesa Sur En	30	35
	Edelweiss	70	38
	Loeffier	60	
	Villa Nolda	50	44
Group IV	Bernina	42	42
	National	40	43
	Laudinella (Self-service)	400	40
Club			
Méditeranée	La Reine Victoria		47

CHAMPFER

Group II	Eurotel	200	
	Chesa Guadalej	75	
Group IV	Bristol	60	
	Granita	25	
Hotel Garni	Primula	30	

APPENDIX II

Summary of Ski Runs (*See rear endpaper map*)

ENGADINE

			Grade	Drop (m.)	Direct length (km.)
Corvatsch	1	Standard			
		(a) to Mandras	★★★	733	2·0
		(b) to Margun Vegl	★★	163	0·5
	2	Fuorcla	★★★	733	2·5
	3	Mandras	★	132	0·5
	4	Lejins	★★	295	1·2
	5	Murtel	★★★	295	1·0
	6	Surlej	★★★	832	3·0
	7	Chastellets	★★★	430	1·5
	8	Giand'Alva	★★	236	1·0
	9	Hahnensee	★★★	871	3·8
Muottas Muragl	1	Muottas Muragl (a)	★	232	1·1
		(b)	★★	232	0·9
	2	Punt Muragl	★★★	714	2·5
Pontresina		Alp Languard	★★★	492	1·5
Diavolezza	1	Bernina draglift	★★	294	1·2
	2	Diavolezza			
		(a) glacier	★	150	0·5
		(b) bottom station	★★	733	3·5
	3	Morteratsch	★★★	1077	9·0
Lagalb	1	Minor	★★★★	783	2·3
	2	Gallerie Minor	★★★	783	2·5
	3	Bernina	★★★	783	2·7
Zuoz	1	Albanas	★★★	610	2·0
	2	Pizzet	★★★	610	2·0
Bivio	1	Camon	★★	430	1·8
	2	Mot Scalotta	★	370	2·0
			Totals	13,013	52·5

ST MORITZ

		Grade	Drop (m.)	Direct length (km.)
St Moritz	Plateau Nair	★	170	0·8
	(a) Eagle's Nest	★★		
	(b) F.I.S.	★★		
	1 Standard (Salastrains)	★★	440	2·0
	2 Standard (St. Moritz)	★	226	1·5
	3 Chantarella	★★	150	0·8
	4 Race	★★★	600	1·9
	5 Mauritius	★★★	600	1·8
	6 Akademiker	★★	440	1·5
	7 Zwetschga	★★★	440	1·4
	8 Opel	★★★	440	1·3
	9 Nater	★★	440	1·5
	10 Olympic	★★★	483	2·0
	11 Rominger	★★	483	2·5
	12 Bushell	★★★	758	3·5
Marguns	13 Flying Kilometre	★★★★	209	0·7
	14 Corviglia-Marguns	★	209	0·8
	15 Plateau Nair—Marguns	★★	315	1·2
	16 Celerina	★★	550	3·0
	17 Trais Fluors: Black	★★★	482	1·5
	18 Red	★★★	482	2·0
	19 Blue	★★	482	2·5
	20 Glüna	★★	541	2·0
Piz Nair	21 Schlattain	★★	778	4·0
	22 Piz Nair to Grischa	★★	309	1·0
	23 Grischa Lift	★★	221	0·8
	24 Saluver	★★★	690	3·0
	25 Suvretta Valley	★★★	1122	6·5
	26 Piz Nair:			
	(a) Face	★★★★	Not official	
	(b) Andrea Couloir	★★★★	Not pisted	
	(c) Guinness	★★★★	Not patrolled	
Suvretta	27 Swing	★★	440	1·5
	28 Paradise	★★	440	2·0
	29 Suvretta House	★★	283	1·0
	30 To Salastrains	★	170	1·3
		Totals	13,393	57·3

Bibliography

Itinera per Helvetiae Alpinas Regiones: Johann Jakob Scheuchzer: Lugduni Batavorum, 1723.

In *Epistolarum ab eruditis viris ad Alb. Hallerum scriptarum, Pars I:* Johann Gesner: Bernae, 1774.

Schweizergeographie: Gabriel Walser: Zürich 1776.

Voyages en differens pays de l'Europe: Carlo Anton Pilati di Tassullo: En Suisse, 1778.

Briefe uber Graubunden: J. F. Heigelin: Stuttgart 1793.

Bemerkungen auf einer Alpenreise uber den Brunig, Pragel, Kirzenberg und uber die Fluela, den Maloya und Splugen: Karl Kasthofer: Bern 1825.

Premiers voyages en zigzag: Rodolphe Topffer: Paris 1844.

La Montagne: Jules Michelet: Paris 1867.

A Season at St Moritz: J. Burney Yeo: Longmans, Green & Co., 1870.

The Playground of Europe: Leslie Stephen: Longmans, 1871.

Holiday Rambles in Ordinary Places by a Wife and her Husband: R. H. Hutton: London, 1877.

Principal Southern and Swiss Health-resorts: William Marcet: London 1883.

The History of Curling: Rev. John Kerr, M.A., F.S.A.Scot.: David Douglas, 1890.

Figure Skating: T. Maxwell Witham in 'Skating' in the Badminton Library: Longmans, Green & Co., London 1892.

Tobogganing on Crooked Runs: Hon. Harry Gibson: Longmans, 1894.

Notes on Tobogganing at St Moritz: Theodore Andrea Cook: London 1896.

De Morbis tartareis 1537: In *Quellenbuch fur die Gemeinde St Moritz:* J. Robbi, Philip Von Hohenheim Paracelsus: Chur 1910.

Early Travellers in tl e Alps: Gavin de Beer: Sidgwick & Jackson, 1930.

British Ski Year Books 1941 and 1942.

Switzerland and the English: Arnold Lunn: London 1944.

Switzerland in English Prose and Poetry: Arnold Lunn: Eyre & Spottiswoode, 1947.

Travellers in Switzerland: Gavin de Beer: Oxford University Press, 1949.

A Singing Reel: Moray McLaren: Hollis & Carter, 1955.

The Swiss and their Mountains: Arnold Lunn: George Allen & Unwin Ltd., 1963.

Beginner's Guide to Curling: Robin Welsh: Pelham Books, 1969.

Index

Compiled by F. D. Buck

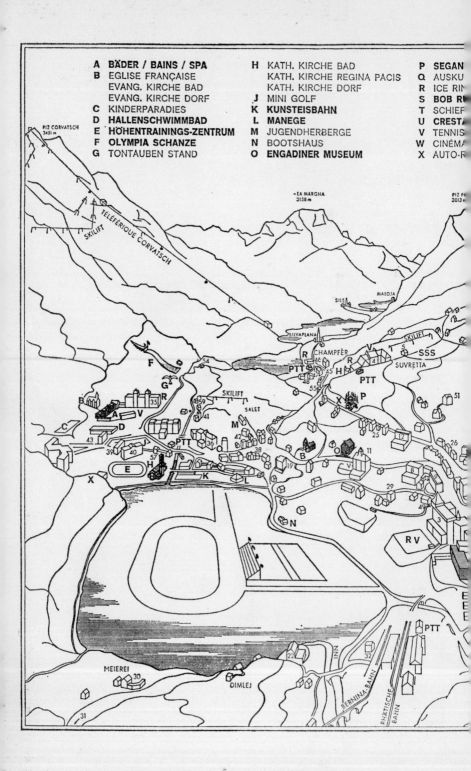

A BÄDER / BAINS / SPA
B EGLISE FRANÇAISE
   EVANG. KIRCHE BAD
   EVANG. KIRCHE DORF
C KINDERPARADIES
D HALLENSCHWIMMBAD
E HÖHENTRAININGS-ZENTRUM
F OLYMPIA SCHANZE
G TONTAUBEN STAND

H KATH. KIRCHE BAD
   KATH. KIRCHE REGINA PACIS
   KATH. KIRCHE DORF
J MINI GOLF
K KUNSTEISBAHN
L MANEGE
M JUGENDHERBERGE
N BOOTSHAUS
O ENGADINER MUSEUM

P SEGAN
Q AUSKU
R ICE RIN
S BOB R
T SCHIEF
U CRESTA
V TENNIS
W CINÉMA
X AUTO-R